Breaking the Chains That Bind Us

Breaking the Chains That Bind Us

Living Life on Life's Terms

The Twelve Steps to Peace, Purpose, and Freedom

Reid Myers

Catholic Deacon, Speaker, and Musician

Frankfort, Kentucky

Paperback ISBN: 979-8-9956330-0-6

Imprint: Breaking Chains Press

Legal Disclaimer

Scripture quotations, if any, are used for inspirational purposes.

This book is intended for educational and inspirational purposes only. It is not intended to replace professional medical, psychological, or counseling advice. Readers experiencing mental health or substance use concerns should seek qualified professional assistance.

References to Alcoholics Anonymous and the Twelve Steps are for educational and informational purposes. Alcoholics Anonymous® is a registered trademark of Alcoholics Anonymous World Services, Inc.

For information about speaking events, workshops, or additional resources, visit:
www.reidmyers.com

First Edition

Printed in the United States of America

JMJ

To Catherine,

for your love, patience, and faith

through every season of our life together.

Table of Contents

Practical Tools

Preface

Why This Book Exists

For many years I have had the privilege of walking alongside people in many different seasons of life.

Through ministry and personal relationships, I have spent time with people in hospitals, nursing homes, recovery meetings, churches, and living rooms — listening to stories of struggle, loss, hope, and healing.

Some were battling addiction.
Some were facing illness or grief.
Some were dealing with broken relationships.
Others simply felt stuck — as if something invisible was holding them back from the life they wanted to live.

Over time I began noticing something important.

Although the circumstances were different, the underlying struggles were often very similar.

People felt trapped by patterns they could not seem to change.

Fear.

Resentment.

Control.

Shame.

Old habits and ways of thinking that seemed impossible to break.

Many of these conversations eventually led to the same place — the principles found within the Twelve Steps.

Originally developed as a path to recovery from alcoholism, the Twelve Steps have helped millions of people around the world find freedom and healing. What many people discover, however, is that these principles are not only for addiction.

They are principles for living.

They offer a practical path toward honesty, humility, responsibility, and spiritual awareness. They help us learn to accept life on life's terms, repair relationships, and live with greater peace and purpose.

More recently, I have begun sharing these ideas through keynote presentations and music, bringing together stories, reflection, and practical wisdom to encourage people on their own journeys.

This book grew out of those experiences.

It is not meant to be a textbook or a set of rigid rules. Instead, it is an invitation to explore a different way of living — one that has helped countless people move from frustration and confusion toward clarity, freedom, and hope.

If you are feeling stuck, discouraged, or uncertain about the path ahead, you are not alone.

And you are not without options.

The journey toward freedom often begins with a simple step: the willingness to look honestly at our lives and consider the possibility that change is possible.

My hope is that the pages that follow will offer encouragement, insight, and practical tools to help you take that step.

Author's Note

Some of the personal stories and examples used throughout this book describe individuals facing challenges related to control, fear, relationships, and personal growth.

The names and identifying details have been changed to protect privacy. Several characters are also composite representations, drawn from the experiences of many people I have encountered over the years through ministry, recovery work, counseling conversations, and personal relationships.

These stories are not intended to portray any specific individual, but rather to illustrate common struggles many people face in life. The goal is to help readers recognize their own experiences and better understand how the principles of the Twelve Steps can apply to everyday living.

The reflections shared from my own life are offered honestly and with humility. My hope is not to present myself as someone who has everything figured out, but simply as someone who has been given a path that has brought healing, freedom, and purpose.

If you recognize yourself in these pages, that is not by accident. The struggles described here are part of the shared human experience.

And the hope offered here is available to anyone willing to begin the journey.

For more resources go to my website:
www.reidmyers.com/life-coaching

Acknowledgments

Many people have influenced my life, and I am deeply grateful for each of them. Without their presence and support, this book would not have been possible.

First and foremost, I give thanks to God, whose grace, patience, and guidance have carried me through both the darkest moments and the brightest blessings of my life. Without that presence, none of the growth I have experienced would have been possible.

To all the friends of Bill W. and Dr. Bob whom I have known over the years — and those I continue to meet — thank you for walking this journey with me.

"In the Fellowship of the Spirit, we walk together as we trudge the Road of Happy Destiny."

The wisdom, honesty, and willingness I have encountered in the rooms of recovery have shaped my life in ways I could never have imagined. So much of what is shared in this book has been learned through those experiences, and I remain deeply grateful for the fellowship that continues to show me a better way to live.

Most importantly, I thank my family.

To my wife, Catherine — your love, patience, and unwavering support over the years have been one of the greatest blessings of my life. Through better and worse, sickness and health, you have been there beside me. Thank you.

To our sons, Jason and Jacob, and our grandchildren, Isabella, Ryan, Alex, and Haley — thank you for the joy and meaning you bring into my life.

And finally, to you, the reader — thank you for taking the time to explore these ideas. Your willingness to grow, reflect, and seek a better way of living gives this message its purpose.

With gratitude,
Deacon Reid Myers

Introduction

A Path to Freedom

If you are reading this book, there is a good chance you are searching for something.

Maybe peace.

Maybe clarity.

Maybe relief from stress or anxiety.

Maybe spiritual growth.

Maybe better relationships.

Maybe freedom from patterns that keep repeating in your life. Or maybe you are simply curious.

Whatever brought you here, I am glad you are here. Because the ideas in this book have changed my life — and the lives of millions of people around the world.

More Than Recovery

Most people associate the Twelve Steps with addiction recovery. And it is true — the steps have helped countless individuals recover from alcoholism, drug addiction, and other destructive behaviors. I am one of those people.

There was a time in my life when alcohol had taken control. My thinking was distorted, my behavior was unhealthy, and my life was moving in a direction that scared me. I reached a point where I needed help, and the Twelve Steps became the path that led me back to sanity, stability, and hope.

But over time I discovered something important. The Twelve Steps are not only about addiction recovery. They are about life. Every human being struggles with fear, control, resentment, relationships, disappointment, uncertainty, and the challenges of simply being human.

The steps address those universal experiences. They provide a practical framework for living with greater peace, responsibility, and purpose.

A Spiritual but Practical Path

This book talks about spirituality. For some readers, that word feels comfortable. For others, it may create hesitation.

Let me reassure you. Spirituality in this context does not mean religion, doctrine, or rigid beliefs. It means connection. Connection with something greater than ourselves.

Connection with truth.

Connection with purpose.

Connection with other people.

The steps invite each person to understand that connection in their own way. No prior belief is required. Only openness.

Why the Steps Work

The Twelve Steps work because they address the root causes of suffering. They teach us to:

Accept what we cannot control.

Take responsibility for what we can.

Examine our patterns honestly.

Repair relationships.

Develop humility.

Build healthy habits.

Strengthen spiritual awareness.

Help others.

These principles are timeless.

They align with psychology, philosophy, and spiritual traditions across many cultures. And they work when practiced consistently.

A Journey, Not a Quick Fix

This book is not about instant transformation. Growth takes time. Change happens gradually. But the process works. Small steps create meaningful change. Progress matters more than perfection.

For Everyone

You do not need to struggle with addiction to benefit from the steps. You only need to be human. If you have ever felt:

Overwhelmed.

Stressed.

Stuck.

Frustrated with yourself.

Hurt by others.

Unsure of your direction.

Spiritually disconnected.

Then the principles in this book can help.

My Hope for You

My hope is simple. That you discover tools that help you live with more peace. That you experience freedom from patterns that no longer serve you. That you develop stronger relationships. That you find purpose in helping others.

And that you realize something deeply important:

You are capable of growth.

No matter where you start.

An Invitation

As you read, take what resonates. Reflect honestly. Practice what you learn. You do not have to do everything perfectly. You only need willingness. The journey begins with a single step.

And that step can start today!

A Simple Reflection Before We Begin

Before you continue reading, I would like to invite you to do something simple. Take a moment and write down one thing about yourself that you would like to change.

Not your job.

Not your spouse.

Not your children.

Not your circumstances.

Just one thing about yourself.

Maybe it is a habit you have tried to break. Maybe it is a reaction you wish you didn't have. Maybe it is something that keeps showing up in your life again and again. Something that may be holding you back.

Write it on the back page of this book or on a separate piece of paper.

Keep it to yourself.

Now ask yourself a few questions.

How long has this been a struggle?

How many times have I tried to change it?

What usually happens when I try?

Now consider one more question.

If it were easy to change, wouldn't I have already done it? Most of us have tried again and again to change certain things in our lives. And yet the same patterns often return. Very often, the thing you just wrote down is one of the chains that has been quietly shaping your life.

This book is about learning how those chains can be broken.

Chapter 1
Owning My Story

If someone had told me years ago that my life would one day become peaceful, meaningful, and full of purpose, I would have quietly dismissed them…or maybe not so quietly.

There was a time when my life felt completely out of control. From the outside, things did not always look that way. Like many people who struggle, I became very good at hiding the truth. I could smile when I was breaking inside. I could sing when my heart was heavy. I could talk about faith while quietly doubting myself.

But inside, something was slowly unraveling. I was drinking more than I ever intended. My thinking was becoming distorted. My relationships were suffering. And the person I saw in the mirror was not the person I wanted to be. I felt trapped. Not just by alcohol. But by my own patterns, fears, and thinking. It was as if invisible chains had quietly wrapped themselves around my life.

Chains of pride.

Chains of fear.

Chains of resentment.

Chains of control.

And the harder I tried to manage everything myself, the tighter those chains seemed to pull. For a long time, I believed the problem was everything around me.

Other people.

Circumstances.

Stress.

Bad luck.

But eventually, I had to face a much more uncomfortable truth. The problem was not only around me. Much of it was inside me. And that realization became the beginning of something I never expected. Freedom.

A Turning Point

My life did not change overnight. Real change rarely happens that way. But there was a moment when I reached a place many people in recovery understand all too well. A place of complete exhaustion. A place of complete helplessness.

I had tried everything I could think of to control my drinking and manage my life.

Promises.

Resolutions.

Willpower.

Denial.

Even prayer.

Nothing worked for long. Eventually, I reached a moment where I could no longer pretend everything was fine. And strangely enough, that moment became the doorway to a new life.

A Path I Never Expected

When I was first introduced to the Twelve Steps, I assumed they were simply a program for people struggling with addiction. And they certainly are that. The Twelve Steps have helped millions of people recover from alcoholism, addiction, and destructive habits.

But over time, I began to see something much deeper.
These steps are not only about addiction. They are about life.

They address the struggles that nearly everyone experiences:

Fear.

Resentment.

Control.

Shame.

Broken relationships.

Spiritual confusion.

They offer a practical path toward honesty, humility, emotional balance, and spiritual growth. In other words, they help us break the chains that quietly shape our lives.

The Chains We All Carry

You do not have to struggle with addiction to feel trapped. Many people feel bound by patterns they wish they could change:

Anger that appears too quickly.

Worry that never seems to quiet down.

Resentments that refuse to let go.

Habits that return again and again.

We promise ourselves we will change. We try harder. And yet the same patterns often return. Why? Because many of the struggles in our lives cannot be solved by willpower alone. They require something deeper.

Honesty.

Willingness.

Humility.

Connection with something greater than ourselves.

That is what the Twelve Steps teach.

And that is what this book is about.

A New Way to Live

This book is not a textbook. It is not a set of rules. And it is not only for people struggling with addiction.

It is an invitation.

An invitation to explore a way of living that has helped millions of people experience greater freedom, peace, and purpose.

The principles you will read about in these pages are simple. But they are powerful. They have transformed my life. And they have transformed the lives of many others.

If you are willing to look honestly at yourself…

If you are open to growth…

If you are searching for a better way to live…

Then this journey may change your life too.

And it begins with a simple step.

Honesty.

Chapter 2

Life on Life's Terms

After beginning my journey of recovery, I started to discover something surprising. When I first got sober in Alcoholics Anonymous, I thought the hardest part of my life was behind me. I was wrong.

Getting sober was hard, no question. I had to face physical withdrawal, emotional instability, and the wreckage my drinking had created in my relationships and career. But what surprised me most was what came after I put the bottle down. Life didn't suddenly become easy. In fact, in many ways, it became more difficult.

Because alcohol had been my way of coping with life — with stress, fear, disappointment, insecurity, and uncertainty. When it was gone, all those things were still there. The difference was, now I had no anesthesia.

I had to learn how to live.

In recovery circles, there's a phrase you hear often: *life on life's terms.* At first I didn't fully understand what that meant. Eventually I realized it meant this:

Life doesn't always go the way we want.

People disappoint us.

Plans fall apart.

We make mistakes.

We get hurt.

We hurt others.

We experience fear, anger, resentment, grief, and uncertainty.

In other words, we experience the normal human condition.

You don't have to be an alcoholic to struggle with life on life's terms. That realization changed everything for me. Because I began to see that alcohol was never really my problem. Alcohol had been my solution — an unhealthy and destructive solution, but a solution nonetheless. It helped me escape feelings I didn't want to feel and situations I didn't know how to handle.

When alcohol was removed, the real issues were still there:

Fear.

Control.

Resentment.

Pride.

Insecurity.

Emotional pain.

Broken relationships.

Spiritual disconnection.

And those are not alcoholic problems. Those are human problems. That's why the Twelve Steps of Alcoholics Anonymous are so powerful. They were created to help people recover from addiction, but what they actually provide is something much deeper — a practical path for emotional and spiritual growth.

The Steps taught me how to take responsibility for my life. They taught me how to repair relationships. They taught me how to let go of resentment. They taught me humility. They taught me courage. They taught me how to trust God.

They taught me how to live with peace instead of constant turmoil.

Most importantly, they taught me that change is possible. Not just behavioral change. Internal change. The kind of change that allows a person to become happier, freer, and more at peace — regardless of circumstances.

Over time, I began to realize something remarkable:
The principles that saved my life in recovery could help anyone live better. I started seeing how the Steps applied everywhere.

In business, leaders who practice honesty, accountability, humility, and emotional awareness create healthier workplaces. Employees who are less burdened by resentment and fear are more productive, more creative, and more engaged. Organizations thrive when people operate from clarity rather than ego.

In families, the ability to admit mistakes, ask forgiveness, and release resentment transforms relationships. Marriages heal. Parents become more present. Children grow up in environments shaped by grace instead of tension.

In faith communities, the Steps provide a practical pathway to spiritual growth. They move people beyond intellectual belief into lived experience — trust, surrender, forgiveness, service, and connection with God.

And on a personal level, the benefits are profound.
Less anxiety.
Less anger.
More peace.
More confidence.
More purpose.
More joy.
Serenity.

The promise of the Twelve Steps is not perfection.
It is transformation.

When I first entered recovery, I wanted my problems to disappear. What I discovered instead was something far better: I began to change. As I changed, my experience of life changed.

Circumstances didn't always improve. But I did. That is the quiet miracle of spiritual growth. You don't have to be an alcoholic to benefit from the Twelve Steps. You only have to be human. You only have to recognize that some parts of life aren't working the way you want them to — and be willing to explore a different path.

This book is about that path.

It's about how the Twelve Steps can help anyone — regardless of background, beliefs, or struggles — live a happier, freer, and more joyous life.

Chapter 3
The Chains That Bind Us

As human beings, we like to think of ourselves as free.

Free to make our own choices.

Free to live the way we want.

Free to shape our own lives.

And in many ways, that is true. But if we are honest with ourselves, most of us eventually discover something uncomfortable.

We are not as free as we think we are.

There are patterns in our lives that seem to repeat no matter how hard we try to change them. Habits we promise ourselves we will break. Reactions we wish we could control. Thoughts that return again and again.

We try harder.

We make new resolutions.

We promise ourselves this time will be different.

And for a while, it often is.

But then something happens. Stress appears. Fear creeps in. Someone disappoints us. Circumstances change. And suddenly we find ourselves reacting the same way we always have. It can feel like something unseen is quietly pulling the strings.

In many ways, that is exactly what is happening.

Invisible Chains

Addiction is one of the most visible chains a person can experience.

Alcohol.

Drugs.

Gambling.

Pornography and sex

But addiction is only one form of bondage.

Many of the chains that affect our lives are far more subtle. They hide beneath the surface. They shape our thinking, our emotions, and our reactions. And most of the time we do not even realize they are there.

These chains can take many forms.

Control

Approval

Success

Comfort

Avoidance

Fear

Resentment

Busyness

Perfectionism

None of these things seem dangerous at first glance. In fact, many of them can appear positive. But when they begin to control our thinking and behavior, they quietly become chains.

The Illusion of Control

One of the strongest chains many people experience is the desire for control. We want life to go according to our plans. We want people to behave the way we expect. We want circumstances to cooperate with our hopes. When things go well, we feel confident.

But when life refuses to cooperate, frustration appears. We try harder. We push. We force. But the harder we try to control everything, the more exhausting life becomes.

Eventually we discover something important:

Much of life is not within our control.

Other people have their own thoughts and decisions.

Circumstances change. Unexpected events occur. And when we cling too tightly to control, life becomes a constant battle.

The Weight of Resentment

Another powerful chain is resentment. Resentment often begins with a real wound.

Someone hurt us.

Someone disappointed us.

Someone treated us unfairly.

Those experiences can leave deep emotional marks.

But when resentment lingers, it begins to harm the person carrying it. We replay the situation in our minds. We rehearse conversations. We imagine what we wish we had said.

The past continues to live in the present.

Over time resentment becomes heavy.

It drains emotional energy. It shapes how we see others. And often it keeps us trapped in pain long after the original event has passed. Resentment is like drinking poison and waiting for the other person to die.

Fear Beneath the Surface

Fear is another chain that quietly influences many lives. Sometimes the fears are obvious. Fear of failure. Fear of rejection. Fear of loss. Other times they are more subtle.

Fear of not being enough.

Fear of being exposed.

Fear of losing control.

Fear of what others may think.

Fear can drive behavior in powerful ways. It can cause us to avoid opportunities. It can push us to overwork. It can lead us to control others. It can cause anger when we feel threatened. Often we do not recognize fear for what it is. We simply experience the reactions it produces.

The Trap of Perfection

Some people are bound by the chain of perfectionism. They believe they must perform perfectly. Mistakes feel unacceptable. Failure feels humiliating. And so they push themselves relentlessly.

At first, this can look like ambition or discipline. But perfectionism often creates anxiety, frustration, and exhaustion. No matter how much is accomplished, it never feels like enough. Perfection becomes a prison rather than a motivation.

Why Willpower Alone Often Fails

Many people recognize these patterns in their lives. They try to change them through determination. They make promises. They create plans. They try to force themselves into better behavior. But willpower alone often fails. Not because people are weak. But because these patterns are deeply rooted. They involve habits of thinking, emotional reactions, and spiritual disconnection that developed over many years. Real change requires something deeper than determination. It requires honesty. Willingness. Humility.
And often, help from something greater than ourselves.

The Beginning of Freedom

Freedom begins with awareness. We must first see the chains before we can break them. That is why the Twelve Steps begin with honesty. They invite us to look at ourselves truthfully. Not with shame. Not with harsh judgment. But with clarity. When we see the patterns shaping our lives, something remarkable happens. We begin to understand ourselves more deeply. And understanding creates the possibility of change.

A Universal Experience

You do not need to struggle with addiction to recognize these chains. Every human being experiences some version of them. Anger that appears too quickly. Worry that refuses to quiet down. Resentment that lingers. Compulsive behaviors that return again and again. These struggles are part of the human condition. But they do not have to control our lives.

A Path Forward

The Twelve Steps offer a path for breaking these chains. Not through force. Not through perfection. But through a process of growth and the building of virtue through these principles:

Honesty.

Faith.

Courage.

Integrity.

Willingness.

Humility.

Love.

Justice.

Perseverance.

Spiritual awareness.

Service.

Step by step, these principles loosen the chains that quietly shape our lives. And over time, something remarkable happens. Freedom begins to grow. But that freedom begins with a simple realization. We cannot change what we refuse to see. That realization leads us to the first step.

And that is where the journey truly begins.

Chapter 4

Powerlessness and the Illusion of Control

Step One

One of the biggest surprises of my life came after I got sober.

I assumed that once alcohol was out of the picture, everything else would fall into place. I thought my relationships would automatically improve, my emotions would stabilize, and life would finally feel manageable. Instead, I found myself overwhelmed.

I was sober — but I was still anxious. Still frustrated. Still afraid. Still trying to control everything around me. That's when I began to understand something I had never fully seen before:

My real problem wasn't alcohol. My real problem was me.

In Alcoholics Anonymous, Step One says:

1. We admitted we were powerless over alcohol — that our lives had become unmanageable.

For years, I believed that statement only applied to addiction. But over time I realized the deeper truth behind it applies to everyone.

Because every human being struggles with control.
We try to control outcomes.
We try to control people.
We try to control circumstances.
We try to control how others see us.
We try to control the future.
We even try to control our own emotions.
And when control doesn't work — which is often — we experience anxiety, anger, resentment, frustration, or fear.

The more we try to force life to go our way, the more tension we create inside ourselves. Control promises safety. But it usually produces suffering.

When Life Feels Unmanageable

David C.

David is successful by most external standards. He has a solid career, a family, and responsibilities that matter to him. But internally, he feels like he's constantly carrying pressure.

At work, he worries about performance and outcomes. When projects don't go according to plan, he feels personally responsible. He becomes frustrated when coworkers don't meet expectations. He replays conversations in his mind long after the day is over.

At home, he wants his family to be happy and stable, but he finds himself irritated when things don't go smoothly. Small inconveniences feel bigger than they should. He has trouble relaxing, even during downtime.
At night, his mind races — finances, responsibilities, the future, what could go wrong. From the outside, his life looks fine. Inside, it feels unmanageable.

If you asked David what the problem was, he might say stress, workload, or circumstances. But underneath it all is something deeper. David is trying to control too much. He's trying to control outcomes that aren't fully his to control. He's trying to manage other people's behavior. He's trying to eliminate uncertainty from life. And the more he tries, the more pressure he feels.

His life isn't falling apart. But internally, it's becoming unmanageable.

Maria L.

Maria is a mother who loves her teenage daughter deeply. Lately, her daughter has been making choices Maria doesn't agree with — friendships she questions, priorities that seem off, attitudes that feel disrespectful.

Maria worries constantly. She tries to correct, advise, and sometimes argue. The more she pushes, the more her daughter pulls away. Conversations become tense. Resentment builds on both sides. Maria feels fear disguised as frustration.

What she really wants is control — control over her daughter's decisions, safety, and future. But she doesn't have that control. And the more she tries to force it, the more painful their relationship becomes.

Rachel W.

Rachel is a person of sincere faith. She prays regularly, attends church, and genuinely believes God is involved in her life. When challenges arise, her first response is often prayer. But over time, she begins noticing something troubling.

She prays for situations to resolve a certain way — for a relationship to heal, for a job opportunity to work out, for a loved one to change, for circumstances to improve. When things unfold differently than she hoped, frustration creeps in.

She wonders why God isn't answering. She feels disappointed. Sometimes even hurt. Quietly, doubt begins to grow. What Rachel doesn't realize at first is that she isn't just trusting God. She's expecting God to do specific things.

In subtle ways, she's trying to control outcomes through prayer. And when life doesn't match those expectations, her faith feels shaken. The deeper struggle isn't spiritual failure.

It's control.

True trust requires releasing outcomes — not managing them. Step One invites us to recognize that even in our spiritual lives, we are not in control. We cannot control timing, circumstances, or how God chooses to work. But when we stop trying to manage everything — even God — something unexpected happens.

Faith becomes less fragile. Peace becomes more possible.

Reid M.
Yep, that's me. By the time I reached Step One, I had nowhere else to go.

My drinking had absolutely crushed me.

I always told myself I could quit whenever I wanted. But when I wanted to, I couldn't — no matter how hard I tried. My life had become a life of despair, a state of *incomprehensible demoralization*, as the Big Book of Alcoholics Anonymous describes it.

It was easy for me to admit I was powerless and that my life had become unmanageable. In a strange way, I can say I was blessed in that respect.

David, Maria, and Rachel haven't hit rock bottom. Maybe they never will. Their situations aren't life and death. Theirs are struggles that feel confusing and frustrating but not catastrophic. So their patterns continue — and so do their struggles.

David, Maria, Rachel, and me.
Different circumstances.
Same underlying struggle.
The struggle for control.

Understanding Powerlessness

Step One introduces a word many people resist: powerlessness. We often associate powerlessness with weakness, failure, or defeat. But that's not what Step One is talking about.

Powerlessness simply means recognizing reality. There are things we cannot control.

Other people's choices.

Outcomes.

Timing.

The future.

The past.

Unexpected events.

Aging.

Loss.

Circumstances beyond our influence.

Admitting powerlessness is not giving up. It's getting honest. It's acknowledging that our strategies for controlling everything are not working. And that honesty creates the possibility for change.

How Control Creates Unmanageability

One of the most important realizations of Step One is this:

Unmanageability often isn't about what's happening around us.

It's about what's happening inside us while we try to control it.

When we fight reality, we create tension.

When we resist uncertainty, we create anxiety.

When we try to control people, we create conflict.

When we demand outcomes, we create frustration.

The harder we grip, the more exhausted we become.

Many people live highly functional lives externally while feeling chaotic internally. You can be successful and still feel unmanageable. You can be responsible and still feel overwhelmed.
You can be accomplished and still feel restless.
Unmanageability is an internal condition. And recognizing it is not failure.

It's awareness.

The Freedom in Surrender

The paradox of Step One is powerful:
Admitting powerlessness is the beginning of freedom.

When we stop fighting what we cannot control, we stop exhausting ourselves. When we loosen our grip, we create space for peace. For me, admitting powerlessness didn't mean I had no responsibility. It meant I was no longer pretending I could control everything.

My life had become unmanageable — not just because of alcohol, but because of how I was trying to live. Step One helped me see that clearly. And once I saw it, I became open to something new:
Help. Hope. A different way of living.
Because once we admit we don't have all the answers, we become willing to look beyond ourselves. That is where transformation begins.

And that is where Step Two enters the picture.

Putting Step One into Practice

Step One begins with honesty — not judgment, not shame, just awareness.

The goal is not to fix anything yet. The goal is simply to notice where control is creating tension in your life.

Exercise: The Control Inventory

Take a few quiet minutes and write down answers to the following:

1. What situations in my life currently cause me the most stress or frustration?

2. In those situations, what am I trying to control?

3. Is that something I truly have control over?

4. How does trying to control it affect me emotionally?

5. What might it feel like to loosen my grip — even slightly?

Awareness alone begins the process of freedom.

A Simple Step One Statement

I am willing to admit that I cannot control everything. I am open to a new way of living.

Optional Prayer

God, help me see where I am trying to control what I cannot. Give me honesty, humility, and the willingness to let go. Help me trust that peace is possible even when life feels uncertain. Amen.

Chapter 5

Hope Is Possible

Step Two

After we admit that we are not in control of everything, a natural question arises: Now what?

If Step One is about honesty.

Then Step Two is about Hope.

In Alcoholics Anonymous, Step Two says:

2. We came to believe that a Power greater than ourselves could restore us to sanity.

For many people, this step can feel uncomfortable at first. The phrase Power greater than ourselves raises questions. Some people immediately think of religion. Others feel resistance because of past spiritual experiences or misunderstandings about God.

But at its core, Step Two is not about religion. It's about possibility.

It's about recognizing that if our own strategies haven't been working, maybe help exists beyond our own limited perspective. It's about moving from isolation to connection.

It's about hope.

Hope is often misunderstood.
We tend to think hope means believing things will work out the way we want. But real hope is deeper than optimism.

As Václav Havel once wrote:
"Hope is not the conviction that something will turn out well but the certainty that something makes sense, regardless of how it turns out."

This kind of hope does not depend on outcomes. It does not require certainty. It does not demand control. It rests in the belief that life has meaning, even when we cannot see it clearly.

Step Two invites us into this kind of hope — the hope that there is a power greater than ourselves at work, even when circumstances feel uncertain or difficult.

When Self-Reliance Isn't Enough

Brian A.

Brian is a hard worker. He genuinely wants to grow, succeed, and become a better version of himself. He reads books on productivity, organization, leadership, and motivation. He watches videos, listens to podcasts, and has even invested significant money in courses and programs designed to help him improve his life.

Each time he discovers something new, he feels energized. This is it," he thinks. "This is what I've been missing."

He creates plans.

He sets goals.

He organizes his schedule.

He starts new routines with enthusiasm. For a while, things improve. Then something happens.

Momentum fades.

The routines slip.

The energy drops.

The excitement disappears.

Before long, Brian finds himself back where he started.

Again.

Each cycle leaves him more frustrated. He wonders why discipline seems so easy for other people. He begins questioning his own character.

Maybe I'm just lazy.

Maybe I don't have what it takes.

Maybe something is wrong with me.

The disappointment turns inward.

What Brian doesn't realize is that his struggle isn't about motivation or willpower.

It's about self-reliance.

He believes that if he just finds the right system, the right strategy, or enough determination, he can force himself into lasting change.

But real transformation rarely comes from self-effort alone.
At some point, sustainable change requires something beyond
personal willpower — support, connection, spiritual grounding,
and guidance outside our own thinking.

When Brian begins to consider that possibility — that help
might exist beyond himself — hope starts to grow.

And hope is where change begins.

Lisa G.

Lisa has struggled with anxiety for years. She analyzes
situations, anticipates problems, and constantly tries to prepare
for what might go wrong. She reads books, listens to podcasts,
and practices techniques to calm herself.

Sometimes they help. But the anxiety always returns. One day,
during a particularly overwhelming moment, she admits
something she's never said before:
I don't know how to fix this on my own.

In that moment, something shifts. Instead of trying harder, she becomes willing to consider that help might exist outside her own mind.

That willingness is the seed of Step Two.

Rachel W.

Or consider Rachel, the woman of faith we met earlier. After experiencing disappointment when life didn't unfold the way she expected, she begins to reexamine what trust really means. Slowly she realizes that faith isn't about outcomes — it's about relationship.

Instead of asking, "Why isn't God doing what I want?" she begins asking, "Where is God in this moment?" Her faith begins to feel less like control and more like connection. Hope grows.

Different people.
Different struggles.
Same turning point.

The realization that we cannot do everything alone.

Understanding a Power Greater Than Ourselves

Step Two does not require a specific religious belief. It simply invites us to recognize that we are not the highest power in our lives. For some people, that Power is clearly God.

For others, it begins with something simpler:

- The wisdom of trusted people

- The support of community

- The laws of nature

- Love

- Truth

- Spiritual presence

- The possibility of growth itself

The key idea is humility.

If our own thinking alone hasn't solved our struggles, perhaps guidance exists beyond our current perspective.

That realization opens the door to change.

Restoring Us to Sanity

The phrase restore us to sanity can sound dramatic, but its meaning is practical. When we repeat patterns that don't work — controlling, worrying, reacting, resisting — we create suffering.

Sanity, in this context, means returning to balance.
Clarity.
Peace.
Emotional stability.
Perspective.

A Power greater than ourselves doesn't necessarily remove problems. But it can change how we experience them.
We become calmer.
More grounded.
More trusting.
Less reactive.

Life feels more manageable.

Hope Is a Turning Point

Step Two is not about certainty. It's about willingness. We move from:

"I have to fix everything myself."

to

"Maybe I don't have to do this alone."

Hope often begins very quietly.

A conversation.

A moment of honesty. A sense of peace during prayer.

A realization that change might be possible. Hope is the bridge between struggle and transformation. And once hope appears, the next step becomes possible:

Trust.

Putting Step Two into Practice

The goal of Step Two is openness — becoming willing to believe that help exists beyond your own control.

You don't need perfect faith. You only need willingness.

41

Exercise: Opening to Hope

Take a few quiet minutes to reflect on these questions:

1.   Where in my life do I feel stuck or overwhelmed right now?

2.   Have my current strategies fully solved this problem?

3.   What might it look like to receive help instead of trying harder?

4.   What does "a Power greater than myself" mean to me today?
(This can be God, love, truth, community, wisdom, or simply the possibility of change.)

5.   Am I willing to believe that change is possible — even if I don't know how yet?

Write whatever comes to mind without judgment.

A Simple Step Two Statement

I am open to the possibility that I am not alone and that help is available to me.

Optional Prayer

God, help me become willing to believe that change is
possible.

Open my mind and my heart to guidance beyond my own
understanding.

Restore me to clarity, peace, and balance.

Amen.

And now we arrive at Step Three — deciding who or what that

Higher Power is for us.

Chapter 6

Choosing Trust

Step Three

If Step One is honesty, and Step Two is hope, then Step Three

is a decision. A decision that involves faith. A decision to trust.

In Alcoholics Anonymous, Step Three says:

3. We made a decision to turn our will and our lives over to

the care of God as we understood Him.

For many people, this step can sound intimidating at first.

Words like turn our will over may create images of losing

control or becoming passive.

But Step Three is not about giving up responsibility. It's about changing how we live. It's about moving from self-reliance alone to a partnership with something greater than ourselves. It's about trust.

The Limits of Self-Will

Most of us spend our lives operating on self-will.

We decide what should happen.

We plan how things should unfold.

We try to manage outcomes.

We push harder when life resists.

Sometimes self-will works. But often it creates tension.

Because life does not always cooperate with our plans.

When outcomes don't match expectations, we feel frustration, fear, disappointment, or anger. We may double our efforts, trying to force things into place.

This becomes a formula for conflict. We push harder, try harder, and force more. Our motives may be good, but the more we push, the more we become like a bull in a china shop — stepping on people's toes, creating reactions, and making everything more chaotic. Eventually we feel completely helpless to do anything about it.

Eventually, if we are honest, we may come to a painful realization:

I don't know how to do this alone.

That realization opens the door to Step Three.

Help!

But if we can't do it alone, where will we find help? Most of us have already tried many things that didn't work.

Maybe we read self-help books that encouraged us to align our will in a new direction. Maybe we reached out to friends or relatives, but they eventually tired of hearing the same struggles while seeing little change — even when we took their advice. Maybe we tried dozens of strategies with limited results.

There is a reason they didn't work. We still relied primarily on ourselves — or on other people. In other words, self-will operating in different forms. The real turning point begins with Step One — powerlessness. This is the only step we must do perfectly: admitting that we are powerless.

That admission leads us to Step Two — coming to believe that a power greater than ourselves can restore us.

For many of us, that Higher Power is God.

Houston, We Have a Problem

Not everyone is comfortable with that word. Some may believe there is no God (atheist). Some may be unsure if there is a God (agnostic). Some may have been raised in a church but carry painful memories or resentments connected to religion.

Others may believe in a God who is harsh, angry, or constantly punishing mistakes. These experiences can create real barriers. But consider this:

If you have worked Step Two honestly — if you came to believe that a power greater than yourself could restore you — what kind of power would that need to be?

It would need to be loving power. If that power is capable of restoring you, it must care about you.

It must desire your healing. It must want your good.

This is the Higher Power we are talking about. If your concept of God is relentlessly judgmental, punishing, and angry, then it may be time to reconsider that image.

My Higher Power — whom I call God — loves me. Cares for me. Wants the very best for me. And holds my welfare in His hands.

I could not turn my life and my will over to anything less.

When Self-Will Reaches Its Limits

David C.

In chapter 4, David C. began to see that so much of his life had become unmanageable and the pressure was building.

David had always believed that if he worked hard enough, planned carefully enough, and stayed disciplined enough, things would work out. For years, that approach served him well. But over time, life became more complicated.

Projects didn't always succeed despite his best efforts. Coworkers didn't meet expectations. Unexpected problems appeared. The more he tried to manage everything, the more pressure he felt. He lay awake at night thinking through scenarios — what he should have said, what he needed to fix tomorrow, what could go wrong next.

He wasn't failing. But he wasn't at peace either. Eventually a quiet realization began to surface: "I can't control everything." And deeper still: "Maybe I was never meant to."

At first, that thought felt frightening. But it also opened a new possibility. If he wasn't meant to carry everything alone, maybe there was help available — something beyond his own effort. For the first time, David began to consider letting go of outcomes he couldn't control and trusting that life could unfold without his constant management.

It was only a beginning.

But it was a beginning of surrender.

Maria L.

Let's revisit Maria L. for a moment.

Maria loved her daughter fiercely. She wanted her to be safe, responsible, and successful. When her daughter began making choices Maria didn't agree with, fear took over. Maria corrected. Advised. Argued. Pleaded. The more she pushed, the more her daughter resisted.

Conversations became tense. Distance grew. Both felt hurt.

Maria believed she was helping. But underneath her efforts was

something else:

Control.

She wanted certainty. Safety. Guarantees. One evening,

exhausted and discouraged, she admitted something she had

never said out loud before:

I can't control her life.

That realization was painful. But it also created space. If she

wasn't in control, maybe she didn't have to carry the entire

burden alone. That night, instead of arguing or worrying, Maria

did something different.

She prayed — not for her daughter to change, but for the strength to trust.

For the courage to let go.

For the peace to accept what she could not control.

It was not perfect surrender.

But it was a step toward it.

Rachel W.

And what about Rachel W.?

Prayer was her first response when problems arose. But over time she began noticing something troubling. She prayed for outcomes — for relationships to heal, for situations to resolve, for loved ones to change. When things unfolded differently than she hoped, disappointment crept in. She wondered why God wasn't answering. Quiet frustration grew.

What Rachel slowly began to realize was this:

She wasn't trusting God. She was trying to manage outcomes through prayer. In subtle ways, she was still relying on control. True trust required something different — releasing outcomes entirely.

Not managing God.

Trusting Him.

As she began to let go of expectations and focus instead on trust, her faith became less fragile.

She wasn't controlling the future.

She was placing it in God's hands.

Different Lives — Same Invitation

David, Maria, and Rachel.

Different circumstances. Same underlying struggle. The limits of self-will. And the same invitation:

To trust something greater than ourselves.

To begin turning our will and our lives over.

When Self-Will Runs Riot

For many years, I believed I was in control. Even when evidence suggested otherwise. My drinking and drug use had begun creating problems — relationships strained, responsibilities neglected, consequences appearing — but I still told myself the same thing many people say:

I can quit whenever I want to. I believed that. Until the day I tried to quit. And couldn't. That realization was terrifying. Because suddenly I saw something I had never fully admitted before: I was not in control.

No matter how strong my intentions were, no matter how sincere my promises, no matter how determined I felt in the moment — I returned to the same behavior again and again.

What I called choice was often compulsion.

What I called control was often illusion.

In Alcoholics Anonymous literature, there is a phrase that describes this condition well: self-will run riot. I was trying to manage life on my own terms, driven by fear, ego, insecurity, and the need to feel okay inside. Alcohol and drugs had become my way of coping with emotions I didn't know how to handle.

And despite my best efforts, I could not stop. Alcohol had me in chains. I was a slave in the truest sense. One of the most humbling realizations of recovery is this:

No human power could have relieved me of my addiction.

Advice didn't fix it.

Willpower didn't fix it.

Intelligence didn't fix it.

Determination didn't fix it.

I had to reach a point of surrender. At the time, it felt like defeat. Looking back, it was grace.   There is another phrase from recovery that once puzzled me but now makes perfect sense: we were beaten and crushed into a sense of reasonableness.

Pain has a way of breaking through denial. When I finally reached the point where I had no answers left, I became willing to consider something I had resisted before:

Maybe I cannot do this alone.

Maybe I need help beyond myself.

Maybe I need God.

That willingness opened the door to surrender.

People often say, "Let go and let God." For years I didn't understand what that meant. Eventually I realized it was not about passive resignation. It was about releasing the illusion that I was in charge of everything.

If I had not gone through that pain — the fear, the consequences, the sorrow — I might never have reached that point of surrender. And without surrender, I would never have discovered the life I have today.

Freedom.

Peace.

Purpose.

A new way to live.

Sometimes the experiences we would never choose become the very things that lead us to transformation. Surrender was not the end of my life. It was the beginning.

Looking back, what felt like defeat was actually the doorway to change. There is a profound statement found in Alcoholics Anonymous Comes of Age that captures this transformation:

"Such is the paradox of A.A. regeneration: strength arising out of complete defeat and weakness, the loss of one's old life as a condition for finding a new one."

At the time, surrender felt like losing. In reality, it was the beginning of gaining everything that truly mattered — freedom, peace, purpose, and connection. I was beginning to break free from my chains.

Most people do not have to reach that level of pain to benefit from surrender. But the principle is the same for everyone. Whenever we cling tightly to control, we create tension and suffering. Whenever we release it, we create space for peace.

What Does It Mean to Turn Our Will Over?

Step Three does not mean we stop making decisions. It means we invite guidance into our decisions. It means recognizing that our perspective is limited and becoming willing to seek wisdom beyond ourselves.

Turning our will over means:

• Letting go of the need to control outcomes

• Trusting that we can handle whatever happens

• Seeking guidance through prayer, reflection, and wise counsel

• Acting with integrity rather than fear

• Accepting uncertainty

It is not passive. It is deeply active. We still take responsibility for our actions. But we release the illusion that we control everything.

Trust Reduces Fear

Much of our need for control comes from fear.

Fear of failure.

Fear of rejection.

Fear of loss.

Fear of uncertainty.

Fear of not being enough.

Trust does not eliminate uncertainty. But it changes our relationship to it. When we trust that we are not alone — that guidance, strength, and support are available — fear loses some of its power. Peace becomes possible even in imperfect circumstances.

The Beginning of Spiritual Growth

Step Three marks the beginning of intentional spiritual living.

We move from:

Self-centered living → Spirit-guided living

Control → Trust

Fear → Faith

Isolation → Connection

We begin practicing surrender daily. Not perfectly.

But willingly. And that willingness opens the door to

transformation.

Putting Step Three into Practice

Step Three begins with a simple decision:

I am willing to trust.

You don't need perfect faith. You only need willingness.

Exercise: The Trust Decision

Take a few quiet minutes and reflect on the following:

1.	What situation in my life currently feels most uncertain or stressful?

2.	What am I afraid might happen?

3.	What am I trying to control in this situation?

4.	What would it look like to release some of that control?

5.	What might trusting God — or a Power greater than myself — look like right now?

Write your thoughts honestly without judgment.

A Simple Step Three Statement

I am willing to trust that I do not have to control everything. I am open to guidance and support beyond myself.

Optional Prayer

God, I offer You my fears, my plans, and my uncertainties.

Guide my thoughts and my actions.

Help me trust that I am not alone.

Give me peace as I let go of what I cannot control.

Amen.

Step Three does not solve every problem.

But it changes how we face them. And that change prepares us

for the next stage of growth: Honest self-examination.

That is where Step Four begins.

Chapter 7
Honest Self-Examination
Step Four - Part 1

Once we become willing to trust — to release some control and invite guidance into our lives — a new question naturally arises: What needs to change?

That question leads directly to Step Four.

In Alcoholics Anonymous, Step Four says:

4. We made a searching and fearless moral inventory of ourselves.

At first glance, this step can sound intimidating. Words like *searching* and *fearless* may create anxiety. Some people worry that self-examination means harsh judgment or dredging up painful memories. But Step Four is not about shame. It's about clarity. It's about understanding ourselves honestly so that change becomes possible. Because we cannot change what we do not see.

Why Self-Examination Matters

Most of us move through life reacting rather than reflecting.

We experience situations.

We respond emotionally.

We repeat patterns.

Often, we blame circumstances or other people for our
struggles. Sometimes those factors do play a role.

But lasting growth requires looking inward as well.

Our fears.

Our resentments.

Our insecurities.

Our expectations.

Our behavior patterns.

Our reactions.

Step Four invites us to examine these areas with honesty and
courage. Not to criticize ourselves. But to understand
ourselves.

The Patterns We Don't See

Karen T.

Karen often feels frustrated in her relationships. She believes people don't appreciate her efforts. She works hard to help others, but sometimes feels taken for granted.

Over time, resentment builds.

What Karen doesn't initially see is her pattern of overextending herself to gain approval. When appreciation doesn't come, disappointment turns into resentment.

Her suffering isn't caused only by others. It's connected to her own expectations and fears. When she begins to see that pattern clearly, something changes. She gains freedom.

Or consider **Brian** again — the hard worker who struggled with motivation cycles. As he reflects more deeply, he realizes his bursts of enthusiasm were often driven by fear — fear of failure, fear of not being enough, fear of falling behind. When fear drove him, exhaustion followed. Understanding that pattern helps him shift toward healthier motivation.

Or consider someone recovering from addiction.

For years, substances may have seemed like the primary problem. But Step Four reveals deeper issues:

Fear.

Resentment.

Shame.

Self-centeredness.

Pain.

Unrealistic expectations.

Emotional wounds.

Alcohol or drugs were often attempts to cope with these deeper struggles. Understanding that truth is not condemning. It is liberating.

Fear and Resentment

Two of the most powerful emotional forces affecting our lives are fear and resentment.

Fear tells us we are not safe. Resentment tells us we have been wronged. Both emotions can dominate our thinking.

They influence decisions.

They shape relationships.

They affect our peace of mind.

When left unexamined, fear and resentment grow stronger.

When examined honestly, they begin to lose power.
Step Four shines a light into these areas. And light changes things.

Self-Compassion and Responsibility

One of the most important parts of Step Four is balance. We are not looking for ways to condemn ourselves.
We are looking for truth.
Sometimes we discover mistakes we made.
Sometimes we discover wounds we experienced.
Sometimes both are present.

Healthy self-examination includes responsibility and compassion. We acknowledge our part where appropriate. We also recognize that we are human beings learning and growing.

This balance creates healing instead of shame.

The Courage to Be Honest

Fear often prevents self-examination. We worry about what we
might find. But honesty is rarely as frightening as avoidance.
When we bring thoughts and patterns into awareness, they lose
some of their power over us. We gain perspective. We gain
choice. We gain freedom.
Step Four is an act of courage — and also an act of hope.
Because we only examine what we believe can change.
We are not searching for perfection.
We are searching for truth.

Spiritual Growth Through Awareness

Step Four is deeply spiritual.
It invites humility.
It invites truth.
It invites openness to transformation.

When we become aware of our patterns, we create space for
God — or a Power greater than ourselves — to work within us.
Growth becomes possible.
Not instantly. But steadily.

Putting Step Four into Practice

You do not need to complete a full life inventory today. Step Four begins with simple awareness.

Exercise: Personal Reflection Inventory

Take some quiet time and reflect on the following areas:

1.	What situations or people tend to trigger strong emotional reactions in me?

2.	What fears do I notice in my life right now? (Fear of failure, rejection, loss, uncertainty, not being enough, etc.)

3.	Are there resentments I am holding?

4.	What patterns do I notice in my relationships or behavior?

5.	Where might I need growth, healing, or change?

Write honestly without judgment.

Awareness is the first step toward transformation.

A Simple Step Four Statement

I am willing to see myself honestly so that I can grow.

Optional Prayer

God, give me courage to see myself clearly.

Help me face truth without fear or shame.

Guide me toward healing, growth, and freedom.

Amen.

We are not searching for perfection. We are searching for truth. And truth prepares us for the deeper work ahead. In the next chapter, we begin looking more closely at the patterns, fears, resentments, and behaviors that shape our lives.

That is where Step Four truly begins to take form.

Chapter 8
Causes and Conditions

Step Four - Part 2

The Inventory

In the previous chapter, we introduced the idea of honest self-examination — the willingness to look at ourselves truthfully so growth can occur.

Now we go deeper.

Step Four is not simply reflection. It is action. In Alcoholics Anonymous literature, there is a powerful statement that explains why this step matters so much:

"Though our decision was a vital and crucial step, it could have little permanent effect unless at once followed by a strenuous effort..."

Step Three is the decision to trust. Step Four is the effort that makes that decision real. Without Step Four, surrender often remains an idea rather than a transformation.

Alcohol Was Only a Symptom

One of the most important insights from recovery literature is this: "Our liquor was but a symptom. So we had to get down to causes and conditions."

For someone struggling with addiction, alcohol or drugs appear to be the problem. But deeper examination reveals something more complex:

Fear.

Resentment.

Insecurity.

Self-centered thinking.

Emotional wounds.

Avoidance.

Unrealistic expectations.

Substances were often attempts to cope with these internal conditions.

The same principle applies to everyone — whether addiction is present or not.

Anger is often a symptom.

Anxiety is often a symptom.

Control is often a symptom.

Burnout is often a symptom.

Relationship conflict is often a symptom.

Step Four helps us look beneath the surface.

Self Was What Defeated Us

Recovery literature often describes the core problem as self-centeredness. For many people, that phrase can sound harsh. But its meaning is simple: When our lives revolve primarily around protecting ourselves — our ego, security, comfort, or expectations — we suffer.

Fear drives us.

Resentment traps us.

Control exhausts us.

Step Four helps us see how these patterns operate in our lives. And seeing clearly is the beginning of freedom.

The Inventory Process

The Fourth Step inventory traditionally examines four major areas:

1. Resentments
2. Fears
3. Relationships and intimacy
4. Harm done to others

These areas cover most of the emotional and behavioral patterns that create difficulty in our lives. The purpose is not self-criticism. The purpose is awareness.

We are discovering patterns so we can change them.

Resentments — The Number One Offender

Resentment is often described as one of the most destructive emotional forces. Resentment keeps us focused on what others did. It replays past pain. It fuels anger and self-justification. It drains emotional energy.

But resentment often hides deeper emotions:
Fear.

Hurt.

Shame.

Disappointment.

And sometimes it hides our own responsibility.

Step Four invites us to examine resentments honestly.

Example: A Resentment Inventory

(Sample worksheets and links are available in the back of the book.)

To understand how this process works, let's look at a real-life type of scenario.

I'm resentful at:

The Internal Revenue Service (IRS)

The Cause:

They garnished my paycheck. I went to get paid and was told my wages had been taken to cover unpaid taxes. I lost two weeks pay!

Affects My:

My self-esteem and pride. It was embarrassing. My co-workers — especially HR and accounting — knew about it. My boss knew about it. It made me feel weak and irresponsible.

It also affected me financially. I worried about paying bills and the mortgage. The stress was constant.

It affected my relationship with my wife. She was angry and disappointed, and our relationship suffered.

Where Was I to Blame:

I hadn't paid my taxes for three years. I kept putting it off. I ignored letters from the IRS because I was afraid. I didn't even open them. My avoidance and fear created the situation.

At first glance, it was easy to be angry at the IRS.

They took my money.

They embarrassed me.

They caused stress in my life.

But when we looked deeper, we see something important.

The resentment was covering fear and irresponsibility.

Our own actions — avoidance, procrastination, and denial — had created the conditions that led to the consequence. That realization was not about blaming ourselves harshly. It was about seeing truth. And truth created freedom.

Instead of staying stuck in anger, we could begin to let the resentment go. We could see our part in the situation and understand that the anger itself was only causing further harm. We could learn from the experience and move forward differently.

This is one of the purposes of Step Four.

We move from:
Blame → Understanding
Resentment → Responsibility
Helplessness → Growth

When we see our part clearly, resentment begins to lose its power over us.

Fear — The Driving Force

It is often said that the alcoholic suffers from a hundred forms of fear. I can certainly relate to that. But in my experience, alcoholics and addicts are not the only ones. Much of the world struggles with fear in many forms. What are we afraid of?

We are afraid of losing what we have.
We are afraid of not getting what we want.
We are afraid of people finding out who we really are.

We fear failure, success, abandonment, helplessness, powerlessness, the unknown — even discovering the truth about ourselves.

Fear touches nearly every part of life.
Fear of failure.
Fear of rejection.
Fear of loss.
Fear of financial insecurity.
Fear of not being enough.
Fear of uncertainty.

Fear often drives behavior without us realizing it.

We avoid situations.

We overwork.

We try to control people.

We procrastinate.

We react emotionally.

Step Four helps us identify fears so they no longer operate unconsciously.

Awareness weakens fear. Trust strengthens courage.

Relationships and Intimacy

Human relationships are complex. We all have patterns in how we relate to others. Sometimes we have been hurt. Sometimes we have caused hurt. Often both are true.

Step Four invites us to examine our relationship history honestly:

Where were we selfish?

Where were we dishonest?

Where were we inconsiderate?

Where did we cause harm?

What patterns do we notice? The goal is not guilt. The goal is growth and healthier relationships moving forward.

Harm Done to Others

This area prepares us for later steps of repair and reconciliation. We examine situations where our actions affected others negatively. We consider:

What happened?

What was my role?

What should I have done differently?

This process builds responsibility without shame.

And responsibility creates the possibility of healing.

Why Step Four Requires Step Three

Looking honestly at ourselves can feel vulnerable.

Without Step Three — trust in a Power greater than ourselves — this step might feel overwhelming. But Step Three provides safety. We are not examining ourselves alone. We are examining ourselves with guidance, compassion, and hope.

Trust makes courage possible.

And courage makes honesty possible.

The Freedom of Truth

Step Four is not about discovering how bad we are. It is about discovering what has been hurting us. When patterns become visible, they lose power. When responsibility becomes clear, solutions appear.

When fear is named, courage grows.
When resentment is understood, forgiveness becomes possible.
Truth leads to freedom.

Moving Forward

If this process feels intimidating, remember:
You do not need to do it perfectly.
You only need willingness.

Many people find it helpful to write their inventory using structured worksheets.

Worksheets corresponding to the areas discussed in this chapter are available for download on my website (information provided at the end of this book).

Writing helps organize thoughts, clarify patterns, and deepen awareness.

Putting Step Four into Practice

Put fear aside. Approaching this step with a clear, almost clinical mindset — rather than an emotional one — often makes it easier.

When talking about fear, there is a quote by keynote speaker Tiamo De Vetori that I often use. He says:

"Fear is the only thing in the world that gets smaller as you run toward it."

Most of us spend our lives running from fear. We avoid uncomfortable conversations. We delay difficult decisions. We ignore painful truths.

But Step Four invites us to do the opposite. Instead of avoiding fear, we move toward it with honesty. And as we do, it begins to lose its power. So run don't walk toward your fears, and you will discover just how small they really are.

Begin simply.

Choose one resentment, one fear, or one situation from your life and write about it honestly. Ask yourself:

What happened?

How did it affect me?

What emotions were involved?

Did I have any part in it?

What might I learn from this?

A Simple Step Four Statement

I am willing to see truth about myself so I can grow and be free.

Optional Prayer

God, give me courage to look honestly at my life.

Help me see truth with compassion and clarity.

Guide me toward healing and freedom.

Amen.

If we are thorough in this process, something important happens. We begin to understand ourselves more clearly. And that prepares us for the next step:

Sharing what we have discovered with another person.

That is where deeper healing begins.

That is Step Five.

Chapter 9
Healing Through Sharing
Step Five

After completing a personal inventory, many people experience a mixture of emotions.

Relief.

Discomfort.

Clarity.

Vulnerability.

Hope.

We have looked honestly at our lives — our patterns, fears, resentments, mistakes, and experiences. Now a new question naturally arises:

What do we do with what we've discovered?

That question leads to Step Five.

In Alcoholics Anonymous, Step Five says:

5. *We admitted to God, to ourselves, and to another human being the exact nature of our wrongs.*

At first, this step can feel intimidating. Sharing personal truths with another person requires courage. But Step Five is where healing begins in a deeper way. Because we were never meant to carry the weight of our lives alone.

The Burden of Secrecy

Many people carry hidden shame.

Past mistakes.

Regrets.

Painful memories.

Embarrassment.

Guilt.

Fear of judgment.

Even people who appear confident often carry internal stories they rarely share. Secrecy creates isolation. Isolation increases suffering. When thoughts remain hidden, they often grow larger in our minds than they truly are.

We assume others would judge us harshly. We assume we are uniquely flawed. We assume we must handle everything alone. Step Five breaks that isolation.

Why Sharing Matters

There are several powerful reasons this step works.

First, speaking truth reduces shame. Shame thrives in secrecy. It weakens in honesty.

Second, sharing creates perspective. When we speak openly with a trusted person, we often realize we are not alone. Others understand more than we expected.

Third, connection heals.
Human beings are relational by nature. Being heard without condemnation creates emotional relief and trust.

Fourth, humility grows.
We recognize that we are imperfect — and still worthy of care and connection.

Finally, spiritual awareness deepens.

Admitting truth to God, as we understand God, invites transformation at a deeper level than self-analysis alone.

A Story of Release

Thomas H.

Thomas had carried regret for years about decisions he made earlier in life — choices that hurt people he loved. He rarely spoke about those experiences. When memories surfaced, he pushed them away.

After completing his personal inventory, he reluctantly agreed to share it with a trusted mentor.

At first, he felt nervous.

What will he think of me?
Will I be judged?

But as he began speaking, something unexpected happened. His mentor listened calmly. Without shock. Without condemnation. At times, the mentor shared similar experiences from his own life. Thomas realized he was not uniquely broken.

By the end of the conversation, he felt lighter — as if a weight he had carried for years had finally been lifted.

The past had not changed.

But his relationship to it had.

That is the power of Step Five.

Many people discover the same thing Thomas did — that the fear of sharing is often far greater than the experience itself.

Admitting to God, Ourselves, and Another Person
Step Five includes three parts for a reason. Admitting to God acknowledges spiritual reality. We are not hiding from the truth. We are inviting guidance and healing. Admitting to ourselves reinforces honesty. We stop minimizing or denying what we see. Admitting to another person creates connection and accountability. Each part strengthens the others.

Choosing the Right Person

Many people wonder who they should share with. The person does not need to be perfect. But they should be:

Trustworthy.

Respectful.

Able to listen without harsh judgment.

Committed to confidentiality.

Emotionally mature.

Possible choices include:

A sponsor or recovery mentor.

A spiritual advisor or clergy member.

A therapist or counselor.

A trusted friend with wisdom and compassion.

The goal is safety and honesty.

The Spiritual Principle of Humility

Step Five deepens humility. Humility does not mean thinking poorly of ourselves. It means seeing ourselves accurately.

We are human. We make mistakes. We have strengths and weaknesses. We are capable of growth. Humility allows transformation.

Pride keeps us stuck.

Freedom Begins Here

Many people report a sense of relief after completing Step Five.

Anxiety decreases.

Shame lessens.

Clarity increases.

Peace grows.

We realize something important:

We are not alone.

We are not beyond hope.

We are not defined by our past.

We are capable of change.

Universal Application

Even outside recovery contexts, this principle applies widely. In families, honest conversations heal relationships. In friendships, vulnerability deepens connection. In workplaces, transparency builds trust. In faith communities, confession fosters spiritual growth.

Human beings heal through truth shared in safe and trusted relationships.

Putting Step Five into Practice

After completing your Step Four inventory, it is important to move into Step Five without unnecessary delay. Many people feel nervous about sharing honestly with another person. That hesitation is natural. But waiting too long often increases anxiety and gives fear time to grow.

In many ways, Step Five is like removing a bandage. It may feel uncomfortable for a moment, but relief comes quickly afterward.

Prolonging the process usually creates more tension than the sharing itself.

The goal is freedom — not perfection.

Guidelines for Step Five

Be Thorough and Honest

Go through your entire Step Four inventory, admitting the exact nature of your actions without minimizing, justifying, or making excuses. Honesty is what creates healing.

Create a Safe Environment

Choose a private, quiet, and comfortable setting where you will not be interrupted. Feeling safe helps you speak openly.

Take the Time Needed

Do not rush through the process. This is meaningful emotional work. Take breaks if needed, but remain committed to completing it.

Focus on Patterns

As you share, notice recurring themes — fears, behaviors, or reactions that appear repeatedly. These patterns provide insight into what needs to change.

Let Go of Secrets

The purpose of Step Five is to release the burden of secrets that create shame and isolation. When truth is spoken openly, many people experience relief, connection, and a deep sense of peace.

You are not sharing to be judged. You are sharing to be free.

A Simple Step Five Statement

I am willing to share truth honestly so I can experience healing and freedom.

Optional Prayer

God, give me courage to be completely honest.
Help me release fear and trust the process of healing.
Guide my words and bring me peace.
Amen.

Chapter 10
Becoming Willing to Change
Step Six

After sharing honestly with another person, many people begin to notice something important. Clarity increases. Patterns become visible. We begin to understand ourselves more deeply — our fears, resentments, reactions, and behaviors.

And naturally, a new question arises: What now? That question leads to Step Six.

In Alcoholics Anonymous, Step Six says:
6. We were entirely ready to have God remove all these defects of character.

At first glance, this step can feel overwhelming. Entirely ready? All defects? Most people do not feel completely ready to change everything at once. And that's okay. Step Six is not about perfection. It is about willingness.

Understanding Character Defects

The phrase defects of character can sound harsh, but it simply refers to patterns that create difficulty in our lives.

Fear.

Resentment.

Dishonesty.

Impatience.

Control.

Self-centeredness.

Avoidance.

Pride.

Anger.

People-pleasing.

Perfectionism.

These patterns often developed as ways to cope with life. At one time, they may even have served a purpose. But over time, they begin to cause suffering. Step Six invites us to become willing to release what no longer serves us.

The Gap Between Awareness and Change

One of the most important truths about personal growth is this: Seeing a pattern does not automatically change it.

We may recognize impatience but still react.

We may understand fear but still avoid situations.

We may know resentment hurts us but still hold on to it.

This gap between awareness and change is normal. Step Six exists to bridge that gap. It helps us move from understanding to readiness.

Resistance Is Human

Many people discover they are not fully ready to let go of certain behaviors. We may cling to anger because it feels protective. We may hold onto control because uncertainty feels scary. We may resist change because familiar patterns feel safe.

Step Six acknowledges this reality. We do not need to force readiness. We need to become willing to become willing. Even a small amount of openness is enough to begin the process of change.

This struggle with willingness is not new.

One of the most famous spiritual figures in history, Saint Augustine, described his own resistance to change with remarkable honesty. In his Confessions, he prayed: "Give me chastity and continence — but not yet."

Augustine wanted transformation. He desired a different life. But he was also attached to familiar behaviors and pleasures. Part of him wanted change, and part of him wanted to delay it.

That tension is deeply human. Many of us experience the same internal conflict.

We want peace — but we hold onto resentment.

We want freedom — but we cling to control.

We want healthier habits — but we resist discomfort.

We want spiritual growth — but we fear letting go of old patterns.

Augustine's story reminds us that willingness often develops gradually. Eventually, he did change. He surrendered fully and became one of the most influential spiritual leaders in history. Transformation began not with perfection…but with honesty about his resistance. Step Six invites the same honesty from us.

We do not have to be completely ready today. We only need to become willing.

Spiritual Cooperation

Step Six introduces an important spiritual principle: Transformation is a partnership. We do not change through willpower alone — we change through willingness and cooperation. We cooperate with growth.

We allow change. We become willing to release old patterns. For people of faith, this may involve prayer and trust in God's guidance. For others, it may involve openness to growth, wisdom, and support beyond their own thinking.
Either way, willingness creates movement.

Growth, Not Perfection

Step Six is not about eliminating every flaw instantly. It is about direction. We begin moving toward healthier patterns.
More patience.
More honesty.
More compassion.
More humility.
More balance.

Growth happens gradually. And that is enough.

Freedom Through Willingness

Many people experience relief in Step Six. Instead of forcing themselves to change, they allow change to unfold. Instead of fighting themselves, they cooperate with growth. Instead of shame, they experience hope.

Willingness opens the door.

Putting Step Six into Practice

Step Six begins with honest reflection about readiness. Ask yourself:

What patterns in my life do I recognize as harmful, limiting, or no longer helpful?

Am I willing to let go of them?

If not, am I willing to become willing?

We do not become entirely ready in a single moment.

Willingness often grows quietly as we continue the journey.

Exercise: Readiness Reflection

1. What behaviors or patterns do I want to change?

2. What fears or resistance do I feel about changing them?

3. What benefits might come from letting these patterns go?

4. What might willingness look like for me right now?

Write openly without judgment.

A Simple Step Six Statement

I am willing to become willing to release the patterns that no longer serve me.

Optional Prayer

God, help me become willing to grow and change.

Remove my resistance and fear.

Guide me toward healthier ways of living.

Amen.

Willingness prepares us for the next step.

Step Seven moves from readiness to action — asking for help in becoming the person we are meant to be.

That is where humility deepens.

And transformation continues.

Chapter 11
Humility and Change

Step Seven

After becoming willing to change, a natural question arises: How does change actually happen?

That question leads to Step Seven.

In Step Six we "Were entirely ready to have God remove all these defects of character."

And now Step Seven says:

7. *We humbly asked Him to remove our shortcomings.*

If Step Six is readiness, Step Seven is action. But this action is different from what many people expect. Step Seven is not about forcing ourselves to change through sheer willpower.

It is about humility.

Understanding Humility

Humility is often misunderstood. Some people think humility means weakness, self-criticism, or thinking poorly of ourselves. In reality, humility means seeing ourselves clearly.

We recognize our strengths.

We acknowledge our limitations.

We accept that we do not have all the answers.

Humility creates openness.

And openness allows growth.

Why We Cannot Change Everything Alone

Many people try to change through effort alone.

We set goals.

We make promises.

We push ourselves.

Sometimes this works temporarily.

But deeper patterns — fear, resentment, insecurity, control — often require more than effort. They require transformation. Step Seven recognizes that lasting change often involves help beyond our own willpower.

For people of faith, this means inviting God's guidance. For others, it may mean openness to wisdom, support, and growth beyond the ego.

Either way, humility creates movement.

A Story of Letting Go

Eric D.

Eric had worked through the previous steps carefully. He had taken an honest inventory of his life and shared it with a trusted mentor. Through that process, he began to see patterns he had struggled with for years — impatience, frustration, and anger when situations didn't go his way.

He genuinely wanted to change.

He had already tried willpower. He had promised himself he would stay calm. But stressful situations still triggered quick reactions. Through Step Six, Eric became willing to let these patterns go. He could see clearly that his anger was hurting his relationships and robbing him of peace.

But willingness alone didn't create change. That realization led him to Step Seven. Eric began to understand something new: I cannot force myself into peace. So he did something different. Instead of trying harder, he practiced humility. He acknowledged his limitations.

He admitted that he needed help beyond himself. Through prayer, reflection, and quiet moments of surrender, he began asking God to remove the anger and impatience that had controlled him for so long.

At first, nothing dramatic happened. But over time, something shifted. He noticed small pauses before reacting. Moments of patience where anger once lived. A growing sense of calm in situations that used to trigger him.

The change was gradual. But it was real. Eric realized that transformation was not something he achieved alone. It was something he allowed. The change came not from force — but from humility and openness.

That is the essence of Step Seven.

Asking for Change

Step Seven invites a simple but profound action: We ask.

We ask for help in becoming the person we want to be.

We ask for patience instead of anger.

We ask for courage instead of fear.

We ask for honesty instead of avoidance.

We ask for compassion instead of resentment.

Asking does not mean passivity.

We still take responsibility for our choices.

But we release the illusion that we control transformation alone.

The Spiritual Principle of Surrender

Step Seven deepens the surrender introduced earlier.

We accept that:

Growth is a process.

We are imperfect.

Help is available.

Change is possible.

Humility removes barriers. Pride creates resistance.

Humility creates openness. And openness allows transformation to occur.

Progress, Not Perfection

Step Seven does not promise instant change. Remember, we have already turned our lives and our wills over to the care of God. And that is not something we do only once.
It is something we practice daily — sometimes hourly, sometimes moment by moment.

God may remove some patterns quickly. Others may take time. And some struggles may remain longer than we would prefer. If every defect disappeared instantly, what would we learn? How would we grow? How would we develop patience, compassion, and humility?

Growth is rarely dramatic. It is usually the result of small daily surrenders. We learn through the process. We grow through the struggle. So do not be discouraged if change feels slow.

God's work in us often unfolds over time — not all at once. And throughout that process, one thing remains certain:
He loves you.

Step Seven does not promise perfection. It invites progress. We may still struggle. We may still react. We may still fall short. But something shifts internally. We become more aware. More patient with ourselves. More open to growth. And over time, patterns change.

Universal Application

This principle applies far beyond recovery. In relationships, humility allows apology and repair. In leadership, humility builds trust and collaboration. In families, humility reduces conflict. In spiritual life, humility deepens connection with God.

Humility is not weakness. It is strength guided by wisdom.

Putting Step Seven into Practice

My Creator,

I am now willing that You should have all of me, good & bad. I pray that You now remove from me every single defect of character which stands in the way of my usefulness to You and my fellows. Grant me strength, as I go out from here to do Your bidding. (P.76 AA Big Book)

Step Seven begins with humility and willingness to ask for help. Reflect on the following:

What patterns or shortcomings do I most want to change?

Where do I feel limited in my ability to change alone?

What might humility look like in my life right now?

Exercise: The Humility Reflection

1. What personal patterns cause difficulty in my life?

2. What emotions or fears keep these patterns in place?

3. Am I willing to ask for help in changing them?

4. What would growth look like for me?

Write openly and honestly.

A Simple Step Seven Statement

I humbly ask for help in becoming the person I am meant to be.

Optional Prayer

God, help me grow beyond my limitations.

Remove the patterns that hold me back.

Guide me toward patience, honesty, and compassion.

Help me become the person You created me to be. Amen.

When humility opens the door to change, something else becomes possible. We begin to recognize the ways our actions have affected others.

And we become willing to repair those relationships.

That is where Step Eight begins.

Chapter 12
Willing to Repair Relationships
Step Eight

As we grow through the earlier steps, something begins to change inside us.

We become more honest.

More aware.

More humble.

More willing.

And naturally, our attention begins to turn outward toward others. We begin to see how our actions have affected other people. That realization leads to Step Eight.

In Alcoholics Anonymous, Step Eight says:

8. We made a list of all persons we had harmed, and became willing to make amends to them all.

This step marks an important transition.

We move from internal healing to relational healing.

Understanding Harm

Harm can take many forms.

Broken trust.

Harsh words.

Neglect.

Dishonesty.

Selfish behavior.

Financial damage.

Emotional wounds.

Unkept promises.

Absence when we were needed.

Or even our presence when we brought harm instead of help.

Sometimes harm was obvious.

Sometimes it was subtle.

Sometimes it was unintentional.

Step Eight is not about self-condemnation. It is about responsibility.

And responsibility creates the possibility of repair.

Why Willingness Matters

Step Eight does not ask us to make amends yet. It asks us to become willing. That distinction is important. Willingness comes before action.

We may feel fear.

We may feel shame.

We may worry about reactions.

We may question whether forgiveness is possible.

These feelings are normal. Step Eight simply asks: Am I willing to consider making things right?
Even small willingness is enough to begin.

A Story of Awakening

Jimmy D.

As he worked through the earlier steps, he began to see clearly how his drinking had affected his family. Missed events, broken promises, emotional distance — things he had minimized before now felt clear.

At first, guilt surfaced quickly. But alongside the guilt came something new: A desire to repair.

For the first time, he thought not only about his own pain, but about the pain others had experienced because of his behavior. That awareness was uncomfortable. But it was also hopeful.

Because if harm could be recognized, healing might also be possible.

Barriers to Willingness

Many people encounter resistance in Step Eight.

Fear of rejection.

Fear of embarrassment.

Fear of reopening wounds.

Fear of consequences.

Fear that forgiveness will not come.

Some worry they are beyond repair. Others worry they will cause more harm by bringing up the past.

Step Eight acknowledges these fears. Willingness does not require certainty.

It means openness despite fear.

Self-Compassion and Responsibility

One of the most important balances in this step is compassion.
We acknowledge harm honestly. But we also recognize that we
were often acting from pain, fear, confusion, or unhealthy
patterns. Understanding does not excuse behavior. But it
prevents destructive shame.
We are human beings capable of growth.
Step Eight is about progress, not punishment.

The List

Making the list is straightforward but meaningful. We write
down the names of people we believe we have harmed.
Family members.
Friends.
Partners.
Coworkers.
Employers.
Clients.
Neighbors.
Ourselves.
Yes — sometimes we have harmed ourselves through choices,
neglect, or self-destructive behavior. That belongs on the list as
well. The goal is honesty not perfection.

Becoming Willing

Some names on the list may feel easy.

Others may feel difficult. For those that feel hard, willingness can begin with a simple thought: I'm not ready yet, but I'm willing to become willing. That openness is enough.

Over time, willingness grows.

Spiritual Growth Through Responsibility

Taking responsibility for harm is a sign of growth.

It reflects humility.

Integrity.

Courage.

For people of faith, this step often deepens spiritual awareness. We recognize our imperfections and our capacity for change. We experience both accountability and grace.

Hope for Healing

Step Eight does not guarantee that every relationship will be restored. But it creates the possibility. And often, the process changes us regardless of the outcome. We become more honest. More compassionate. More responsible.

That transformation itself is healing.

The List Is Often Already There

Many people are surprised to discover that they do not need to start Step Eight from scratch. Much of this list has already begun to form during Step Four.

As we examined resentments, fears, relationships, and harms done to others, names naturally appeared. Step Eight is often a matter of reviewing what has already been revealed and organizing it into a clear list.

This step is less about new discovery and more about willingness.

Looking Across Our Whole Life

It is also important to look beyond recent history. Step Eight invites us to consider our entire lives.

Childhood.

Adolescence.

Early adulthood.

Relationships.

Work.

Family.

Friendships.

For those who have struggled with addiction, this means looking not only at behavior during the period of active use — what recovery literature sometimes calls "the madness" — but also at patterns that existed long before substances entered the picture.

Many of the behaviors we regret did not begin with alcohol or drugs. They often grew out of fear, insecurity, anger, or self-centered thinking that had been developing for years. Substances may have intensified the damage, but the underlying patterns were already present.

Recognizing this can actually be freeing. It reminds us that we are not dealing with isolated mistakes. We are addressing lifelong patterns — and lifelong growth is possible.

Step Eight is not limited to a season of life.

It is about becoming willing to repair harm wherever and whenever it occurred.

A Simple Step Eight Statement

I am willing to take responsibility for my actions and consider repairing the harm I have caused.

Optional Prayer

God, give me courage to see where I have hurt others.
Help me become willing to make things right.
Guide me with wisdom, compassion, and humility. Amen.
Willingness prepares us for action.

Step Nine is where healing begins to take place in real relationships.

That is where courage becomes visible.
And where freedom deepens.

Chapter 13
Making Amends
Step Nine

After becoming willing to repair the harm we have caused, the next step becomes clear.

We take action.

In Alcoholics Anonymous, Step Nine states:

9. We made direct amends to such people wherever possible, except when to do so would injure them or others.

This step is where courage becomes visible.
It is also where freedom deepens in ways many people never expect.

What Amends Really Means

Amends is more than saying "I'm sorry." An apology acknowledges regret. An amends demonstrates change.
Amends involve:

Taking responsibility.

Acknowledging harm.

Expressing sincere remorse.

Making things right where possible.

Changing behavior moving forward.

The goal is not to erase the past. The goal is to repair what can be repaired and live differently going forward.

Why Amends Matter

Unresolved guilt and shame can weigh heavily on the mind and heart.

We replay memories.

We avoid people.

We carry regret.

Amends breaks that cycle.

They transform:

Avoidance → Courage

Shame → Responsibility

Regret → Growth

When we take responsibility, we reclaim integrity.

And integrity creates peace.

A Story of Courage

Michael M.

Michael had avoided his brother for years after borrowing money he never repaid. The longer he avoided the conversation, the more uncomfortable it became.

After working through the earlier steps, he became willing to address it. With nervousness, he reached out. He acknowledged what he had done. He expressed sincere regret. He offered repayment. His brother's response was warmer than he expected. Even if it had not been, Michael still would have gained something important: Freedom from avoidance. The conversation changed both of them.

Fear Is Normal

Many people feel fear before making amends.

Fear of rejection.

Fear of anger.

Fear of embarrassment.

Fear of consequences.

These fears are understandable. But remember what speaker Tiamo De Vettori once said, "Fear is the only thing in the world that gets smaller as you run toward it."

Step Nine does not require certainty of outcome. It requires willingness to act with honesty and humility. We cannot control how others respond. We can control our sincerity.

Seeking Guidance Before Making Amends

Before going out to make amends, it is often wise to consult with a trusted advisor — ideally the same person who heard your Step Five, if that is possible.

Many people feel a surge of motivation at this stage. After gaining awareness and willingness, we may feel eager to clean up the past quickly. While that enthusiasm is understandable, moving too fast can sometimes cause more harm than good.

Step Nine is not about relieving our discomfort as quickly as possible. It is about repairing harm in a thoughtful and responsible way. We must remember that we are doing this primarily for the people we have harmed. Yes, we benefit from freedom and relief.But the purpose of amends is learning to live differently — moving beyond selfishness and self-centeredness and becoming more considerate of others, what recovery literature calls "our fellows."

That means putting aside our own desires for relief, forgiveness, or approval. It also means releasing expectations. We may not receive the response we hope for.

Some people may forgive us quickly.

Some may need time.

Some may not respond positively at all.

Some may be angry or hostile.

Their response is not our responsibility. Our responsibility is to make an honest effort to repair harm wherever possible. If someone does not accept our amends, that is okay. We have done our part.

As recovery wisdom often says, our job is to keep our side of the street clean. Guidance helps us determine the best course of action. A trusted advisor can help us consider questions such as:

Is this a person I should make amends to?

Is this the right time?

Would contact cause more harm?

What approach would be most respectful?

Sometimes the answer is yes — move forward.

Sometimes the answer is not yet — more time is needed.

Sometimes the answer is no — direct contact may not be appropriate.

Seeking guidance is not hesitation. It is wisdom. And wisdom helps ensure that our efforts truly support healing rather than unintentionally causing new harm.

When Direct Amends Are Not Possible

Sometimes direct contact is not appropriate.

A person may have passed away.

Contact may cause emotional harm.

Safety may be an issue.

Relationships may be fragile.

In those situations, indirect amends may be appropriate.

Writing a letter without sending it.

Making restitution anonymously.

Changing behavior toward others.

Living differently moving forward.

The spirit of the step matters more than the specific method.

Making Amends to Those Who Have Passed Away

Sometimes the people we have harmed are no longer living. In families especially, anger and resentment can grow over time. Distance develops. Words go unspoken. Apologies are delayed. Pride keeps us silent. And before we know it, the opportunity to speak face-to-face is gone.

When we reach Step Nine and begin considering amends, the weight of this reality can feel heavy. Guilt may surface. Regret may deepen. We may think:

It's too late.

I missed my chance.

Now I just have to live with this.

But do not despair. Even when direct amends are no longer possible, healing still is. Many people in recovery have faced this situation. And there is a meaningful way to make amends when someone has passed away.

One powerful approach is to write a letter.

In that letter express your sorrow honestly. Acknowledge specific wrongs revealed in your Fourth Step.

Admit where you were at fault without excuses. Say what you would say if they were sitting in front of you. Speak the words that were never spoken.

Take your time. Be sincere. Be specific. After writing the letter, you may choose a symbolic act of release. If your loved one is buried nearby, you might visit their gravesite. Bring a non-flammable container. Read your letter aloud. Then safely burn it and allow the smoke to rise — as a symbolic act of letting go.

If visiting a grave is not possible, you can do this in your backyard or in a meaningful place that allows quiet reflection. The act itself is not magic. The healing comes from honesty, humility, and release. You are not sending smoke into the sky. You are releasing guilt from your heart.

 This kind of amends does not change the past. But it can change your relationship to it.
It allows you to grieve.
It allows you to take responsibility.
It allows you to seek peace.
And sometimes, that peace is the amends.

Living Amends

Some of the most powerful amends are lived over time.

Consistent honesty.

Reliability.

Kindness.

Presence.

Responsibility.

When behavior changes consistently, trust can rebuild.

Living amends demonstrate transformation.

Self-Forgiveness

As we make amends to others, something else often happens.

We begin to forgive ourselves. We recognize that:

We were imperfect.

We made mistakes.

We are growing.

We are changing.

Self-forgiveness does not excuse past behavior. It

acknowledges transformation.

And that brings peace.

Spiritual Growth Through Action

Step Nine deepens humility and faith.

We act despite fear.

We trust the process.

We release outcomes.

For people of faith, this step often strengthens spiritual connection.

We experience guidance, courage, and grace in real time.

Freedom on the Other Side

Many people describe a sense of lightness after making amends.

Less anxiety.

Less shame.

More confidence.

More peace.

The past no longer holds the same power.

We move forward with integrity.

Putting Step Nine into Practice

Choose one person from your Step Eight list where making amends feels appropriate and safe. Consult with a trusted advisor if possible, and plan thoughtfully.

Consider:

What happened?

What harm was caused?

What responsibility is mine?

What would repair look like?

Then act with sincerity.

Remember, this is an amends — not just an apology.

As a reminder, amends involve:

Taking responsibility.

Acknowledging harm.

Expressing sincere remorse.

Making things right where possible.

Changing behavior moving forward.

Exercise: Preparing for an Amends Conversation

1. What specifically did I do?

2. How might it have affected the other person?

3. What do I want to express?

4. What action could help repair the harm?

5. Am I prepared to accept any response?

Write your thoughts before reaching out.

A Simple Step Nine Statement

I am willing to take responsibility and repair harm wherever possible.

Optional Prayer

God, give me courage to make things right.
Help me act with honesty and humility.
Guide my words and my actions.
Grant peace to those I have harmed and to me.
Amen.

As we repair relationships, something remarkable happens.
Our lives begin to feel more stable. More peaceful. More grounded. We are no longer running from the past. We are living in the present. That prepares us for the next step: Learning how to maintain growth and emotional balance over time. That is Step Ten.

Chapter 14

Living in Growth

Step Ten

After working through the previous steps, many people experience significant change. Relationships improve. Peace increases. Self-awareness grows. Fear begins to loosen its grip.

But life does not suddenly become perfect.

Challenges still arise.

Emotions still fluctuate.

Mistakes still happen.

That reality leads to Step Ten.

In Alcoholics Anonymous, Step Ten says:

10. We continued to take personal inventory and when we were wrong promptly admitted it.

Step Ten is about maintenance. It is how we sustain growth over time.

A Daily Practice

Earlier steps involved looking at the past. Step Ten focuses on the present moment. We begin paying attention to our thoughts, emotions, and behaviors as life unfolds. When we notice resentment building, we address it. When we make mistakes, we acknowledge them. When fear appears, we recognize it.

Instead of allowing problems to accumulate, we handle them quickly. This prevents emotional buildup.

Perseverance and New Habits

The primary spiritual principle of Step Ten is perseverance.

Growth does not happen all at once. It develops through consistent effort over time. Small daily actions — practiced repeatedly — become habits. And habits shape our character.

Step Ten is where we begin building new habits that support peace, honesty, humility, and emotional balance.

Nuns With wild Habits

There is a a story I heard about these old religious sisters:

A group of elderly nuns lived on the third floor of a convent. Their clothing — their religious habits — were very old, worn, and frayed from years of use. One night a fire broke out on the floor below them, and they could not escape through the building.

The Mother Superior instructed the sisters to tie their habits together into a rope. They secured it to a radiator, lowered it out the window, and one by one climbed safely down to the sidewalk below.

As they stood watching the convent burn, a firefighter approached them in amazement.
"I saw the rope you made out of those old habits," he said. "Weren't you afraid it would break?"

The Mother Superior smiled and replied, "Young man, don't you know old habits are hard to break?"

I suppose you could call this a true story because it's true!
Old habits are hard to break!

Habits — whether good or bad — become strong through
repetition. In the past, many of us developed habits that hurt us:

Avoidance.

Anger.

Dishonesty.

Fear-driven reactions.

Self-centered thinking.

Step Ten is where we begin building new habits:

Honesty.

Responsibility.

Self-awareness.

Humility.

Compassion.

Prompt correction when we are wrong.

Over time, these new habits become strong enough to support
us — even during stressful moments. Consistency creates
stability. Stability creates peace.

Progress, Not Perfection

Step Ten does not expect perfection. Human beings make

mistakes. We react emotionally. We misunderstand situations.

We fall short. The difference now is awareness.

We notice sooner.

We correct sooner.

We learn sooner.

Growth becomes continuous rather than occasional.

Promptly Admitting Mistakes

One of the most powerful aspects of Step Ten is learning to

admit when we are wrong. Promptly.

Without defensiveness.

Without excuses.

Without delay.

This may involve: Apologizing. Clarifying misunderstandings.

Taking responsibility. Making small corrections.

Prompt action prevents resentment and guilt from growing. It

also strengthens relationships.

Emotional Balance

Step Ten supports emotional stability. By addressing issues quickly, we avoid carrying emotional burdens for long periods. We become less reactive.

More thoughtful.

More grounded.

Over time, emotional resilience increases.

A Simple but Powerful Example

As a recovered alcoholic, it is very important for me to promptly admit my mistakes and make amends as soon as possible.

Step Ten keeps me spiritually and emotionally healthy by preventing small incidents from turning into bigger problems.

For Example

One afternoon, I purchased a cabinet hinge from a hardware store. It was packaged individually. When I got home, I realized it was the wrong type. Fortunately, I found another hinge in my toolbox that worked just fine, so I decided to return the one I had just bought.

When I brought it back to the store, the employee told me that the hinges were sold in pairs and could not be returned individually — even though I was certain I had purchased just one. We began going back and forth.

I was already under pressure. My wife and I were preparing our house to sell and in the middle of negotiating for a new car. Stress was high. And in that moment, something small felt big. I lost my cool.

I said a few choice words I shouldn't have said. I tossed the hinge onto the counter. And I walked out in a huff. Later, as my wife and I sat at the car dealership waiting to hear from the manager about our offer, the incident replayed in my mind. Not the argument. My behavior. I felt embarrassed.

Those employees were just doing their job. I had taken their policy personally, as though they were accusing me of stealing. In reality, I had grabbed the hinge in a hurry without checking the packaging carefully. My pride had been wounded.
My ego had flared. My self-esteem felt threatened. But the truth was simple: I was wrong.

That's Step Ten in action.

"Continued to take personal inventory and when we were wrong promptly admitted it." I turned to my wife and said, "I'll be right back."

I drove back to the hardware store.

I apologized for my behavior. I told them I had been out of line and that they were simply doing their job. They looked at me like I was crazy! I don't think they had ever had an angry customer come back to apologize.

But that didn't matter.

I left lighter.

Happier.

At peace.

The situation was small. The freedom was not. That is how these steps work.

Step Ten keeps short accounts.

It prevents resentment from taking root.

It turns small mistakes into opportunities for growth.

It builds the habit of humility. This is perseverance in action.

Recognizing Growth

Step Ten is not only about correcting mistakes. It also includes recognizing growth.

Moments of patience.

Acts of kindness.

Healthy decisions.

Emotional regulation.

Honest communication.

Acknowledging progress builds confidence and motivation.

A Story of Daily Practice

Debbie K.

In the past, Debbie often held onto resentment when coworkers frustrated her. She would replay situations in her mind and carry irritation for days.

After practicing Step Ten, she began noticing those feelings sooner. Instead of letting resentment grow, she addressed concerns calmly or chose to release them.

When she reacted poorly, she apologized quickly. Her relationships improved. Her stress decreased. Life felt lighter. Not because problems disappeared — but because she handled them differently.

Spiritual Awareness

For many people, Step Ten deepens spiritual connection. We become more aware of guidance, intuition, and inner peace. We notice when we are out of alignment. We return more quickly. Daily awareness strengthens trust.

Living with Integrity

Integrity means alignment between values and behavior. Step Ten helps maintain that alignment.

We help others.

We act honestly.

We take responsibility.

We grow.

Integrity creates self-respect. And self-respect creates peace.

Freedom Through Consistency

Small daily actions produce large long-term change.

Checking our behavior.

Admitting mistakes.

Practicing humility.

Choosing kindness.

Over time, these habits create a stable, peaceful life.

Freedom is maintained through consistency.

Putting Step Ten into Practice

Step Ten can be practiced daily with simple reflection. At the end of the day, ask yourself: Did I experience resentment today?

Was I fearful or anxious?

Did I act selfishly or dishonestly?

Did I handle situations with integrity?

Do I owe anyone an amends?

What did I do well today?

Write these things down if it helps. (A mini 4th step)

The goal is awareness, not judgment.

A Simple Step Ten Statement

I am willing to grow daily and correct mistakes quickly.

Optional Prayer

God, help me stay aware and honest.

Show me where I can grow.

Give me humility to admit mistakes and courage to change.

Guide me toward peace and integrity.

Amen.

As we practice daily awareness, something else develops. We become more connected spiritually. We begin seeking guidance regularly. That leads to the next step:

Deepening conscious connection through prayer and reflection.

That is Step Eleven.

Chapter 15

Conscious Connection

Step Eleven

As we practice daily awareness and growth, something begins to change within us. We feel more stable. More grounded. More present.

But many people also notice a deeper desire emerging. A desire for connection. That longing leads to Step Eleven.

In Alcoholics Anonymous, Step Eleven says:

11. We sought through prayer and meditation to improve our conscious contact with God as we understood Him, praying only for knowledge of His will for us and the power to carry that out.

Step Eleven is about relationship.

Not rules.

Not perfection.

Relationship.

Understanding Spiritual Connection

Spiritual connection means different things to different people. For some, it is a relationship with God. For others, it is a sense of meaning, purpose, or presence beyond themselves. For others still, it may be connection with truth, love, or wisdom.

The language may differ. The experience is similar. We feel less alone. We feel guided. We feel supported.

Step Eleven invites us to nurture that connection intentionally.

Prayer and Meditation

Step Eleven mentions two primary practices: Prayer and meditation.

Prayer is often understood as speaking — expressing thoughts, gratitude, fears, or requests.
Meditation is often understood as listening — quieting the mind and becoming aware.

Together, they create balance. Communication and listening. Expression and stillness.
Connection deepens through both.

Improving Conscious Contact

The phrase conscious contact is important. Many people believe spiritual connection should feel dramatic or mystical. Often, it is quiet.

A sense of calm.

A moment of clarity.

An intuitive nudge.

A feeling of peace.

A shift in perspective.

As we practice regularly, awareness increases.

Connection becomes more noticeable.

Guidance and Trust

Step Eleven encourages us to seek guidance: Knowledge of what is right. Strength to carry it out. We do not always receive immediate answers. But over time, patterns emerge.
We recognize wisdom more easily.
We feel more confident making decisions.
We trust the process of life more.

Guidance becomes experiential.

A Story of Stillness

Consider a fellow named **Daniel.**

Daniel lived a fast-paced life filled with constant activity. His mind rarely slowed down. When he first tried meditation, he felt restless and impatient. But he continued practicing for a few minutes each day.

Gradually, he noticed small changes. Moments of calm. Less reactivity. Clearer thinking. During stressful situations, he found himself pausing before reacting. The external world had not changed. But his internal experience had.

That is the power of conscious connection.

Spiritual Growth for Everyone

Step Eleven is not limited to any religious tradition. People of many backgrounds practice forms of prayer, reflection, or meditation. What matters is intention. We create space for connection. We become receptive.

We listen.

The Power of Quiet

Modern life is filled with noise. Constant information. Constant stimulation. Constant activity. Quiet moments allow awareness to grow. Even a few minutes each day can create significant change over time.

Gratitude and Presence

Many people discover gratitude naturally through Step Eleven. We notice small blessings. Moments of kindness. Simple beauty. Gratitude shifts our perspective.

We become more present.
And presence creates peace.

Spiritual Alignment

As connection deepens, behavior often changes naturally.
We become more patient.
More compassionate.
More honest.
More peaceful.
We align more closely with our values.
This alignment creates integrity and purpose.

A Practical Tool: The Daily Examen

Many people find it helpful to have a simple structure when beginning prayer or reflection. One practice that has helped countless people deepen spiritual awareness is the Examen, developed by Saint Ignatius of Loyola.

The Examen is not complicated. It is a way of reviewing the day with openness, gratitude, and honesty, while becoming more aware of God's presence and guidance. It can be practiced in just a few minutes.

The process often includes five movements:

Gratitude

Take a moment to thank God for the day — for moments of connection, help, beauty, or insight.

"God, I thank you for the times this day we have been together and worked together."

Seeking Light

Ask for awareness and clarity.

"God, where have I felt your presence, seen your face, heard your word this day?"

Reviewing the Day

Reflect on experiences, emotions, and moments that stood out.

"With my God, I review the day. I look for the stirrings in my heart and the thoughts that God has given me this day."

Forgiveness and Healing

Acknowledge mistakes or burdens and ask for release.

"I ask for the healing touch of the forgiveness of God who, with love and respect for me, removes my heart's burdens."

Looking Ahead

Consider tomorrow with hope and guidance.

"I ask God to show me how tomorrow might go. I ask for help with any moments I foresee that might be difficult."

At its heart, the Examen reminds us of a simple spiritual truth: "You accept me the way I am and You allow me to grow. You give me time and grace, opportunity, and space."

Practices like this transform prayer from an obligation into a relationship. They help us move from talking about God to walking with God.

As Father Timothy Gallagher writes:
"But what is so utterly foreign to many is the experience of falling in love with God… a response to a God who holds out a hand to say, 'Let's have an adventure!'"

The Power of Silence
Silence also plays a critical role in spiritual life. In a noisy world, quiet moments allow clarity to emerge.

As Cardinal Robert Sarah wrote:
"The greatest things are accomplished in silence—not in the clamor and display of superficial eventfulness, but in the deep clarity of inner vision; in the almost imperceptible start of decision, in quiet overcoming and hidden sacrifice."

Silence is not emptiness. It is space for awareness. Space for guidance. Space for connection. And over time, that connection grows. But silence is not easy. Not in the modern world.

There seems to be noise everywhere all the time. We get so used to it that when it's gone, the world seems strange, and we feel uneasy.

The Monastery

There is a monastery near me — The Abbey of Our Lady of Gethsemani, home of the Trappist monks, the monastery where Thomas Merton lived and wrote.

It is a beautiful place for silent retreat. I try to go there regularly for three days of quiet.
For the most part, the only sound is the chanting of the monks praying the Divine Office seven times a day and the daily Mass. The rest is silence — even during meals.

My first day there is always uncomfortable. I am so used to noise that the silence feels deafening. Thankfully, there are trails to walk and nature all around. That helps release nervous energy. But by the second day, something shifts. I begin to settle into the silence. The prayers slow me down. Spiritual reading deepens. By the third day, I spend long stretches simply sitting and listening — to nature, to stillness, to God.

Mother Teresa once said, "God speaks to us in the silence of our hearts."
That is true.

But we must place ourselves where silence is possible.
Daily quiet.
Time in nature.
Moments away from constant noise.
Only then can we truly hear.

Putting Step Eleven into Practice

Step Eleven can begin with simple daily practices. Choose what feels comfortable and meaningful.

Prayer or Reflection

Speak honestly — gratitude, concerns, hopes, or requests for guidance.

Quiet Time or Meditation

Spend a few minutes in silence, focusing on breathing or simply observing thoughts without judgment.

Daily Intention

Ask yourself: What would living with wisdom or love look like today?

Exercise: Connection Reflection

1. When do I feel most connected or peaceful?

2. What practices help me slow down and listen?

3. What guidance might I need right now?

4. How can I create a few minutes of quiet each day?

Write openly.

A Simple Step Eleven Statement

I am open to guidance, peace, and connection beyond myself.

Optional Prayer

God, help me grow in awareness and connection.

Guide my thoughts and actions.

Give me clarity and peace.

Help me live with purpose and love.

Spiritual growth naturally leads outward.

When we experience healing, we feel a desire to share it. We

help others. We live with purpose beyond ourselves.

That is the final step.

Step Twelve.

Chapter 16
Living with Purpose
Step Twelve

After experiencing healing, growth, and connection, something new begins to emerge.

A desire to help others.

Not out of obligation.

But out of gratitude.

That desire leads to Step Twelve.

In Alcoholics Anonymous, Step Twelve says:

12. Having had a spiritual awakening as the result of these steps, we tried to carry this message to others, and to practice these principles in all our affairs.

This step brings the journey full circle.

Growth becomes service.

What Is a Spiritual Awakening?

A spiritual awakening does not necessarily mean a dramatic moment. For many people, it is gradual.

We think differently.

We react differently.

We live differently.

We experience:

More peace.

More patience.

More awareness.

More compassion.

More purpose.

We begin to see life through a new perspective.

That is spiritual awakening.

Helping Others

Step Twelve emphasizes helping others.

In recovery settings, this may involve sponsorship or sharing experience. But the principle applies universally. Helping can mean:

Listening to someone who is struggling.

Encouraging a friend.

Mentoring a coworker.

Supporting family members.

Volunteering.

Offering kindness.

Service does not require perfection. It requires willingness.

Why Helping Others Helps Us

There is a powerful paradox in human experience: Helping others strengthens us. Service restores balance. When we focus only on ourselves, problems often feel larger. When we help others, perspective changes. We feel connected. Valued. Purposeful.

Service supports emotional and spiritual health.

Practicing Principles in All Our Affairs

Step Twelve is not limited to specific situations. It invites us to live differently everywhere.

At home.

At work.

In relationships.

In communities.

In daily interactions.

We practice:

Honesty.

Humility.

Compassion.

Responsibility.

Patience.

Forgiveness.

Integrity.

These principles become part of our identity.

Living the Principles

Each of the Twelve Steps is associated with a spiritual principle. In order, they are:

1. Honesty
2. Hope
3. Faith
4. Courage
5. Integrity
6. Willingness
7. Humility
8. Brotherly Love
9. Justice
10. Perseverance

11.Spiritual Awareness

12.Service

These principles are not abstract ideas. They are ways of living. As we practice them consistently, they begin to shape our thoughts, our relationships, and our reactions to life.

The final principle — service — often becomes one of the most powerful tools for emotional and spiritual health.

Service Changes Perspective

There is something important I have learned from personal experience.

When I am feeling down or depressed…

When I am hurting — physically, mentally, or spiritually…

My natural tendency, like most people, is to focus on myself.

And the more I focus on myself, the more I suffer.

The more I suffer, the more I feel sorry for myself.

Recovery principles remind me that staying trapped in self-pity only deepens the pain.

We call this sitting on the "pity pot."

So when I notice myself slipping into that place, I try to do something different.

I reach out to someone else.

A Simple Act of Service

One of the things I like to do is pick up the phone and call someone — preferably someone I haven't talked to in a while. It might be an old friend. A family member. A new acquaintance. Someone who simply comes to mind. Before I call, I may ask God to guide me toward whoever might need encouragement. The purpose of the call is not to vent about my problems.

In fact, I don't even mention my struggles at all. It's not the place or time. I call to ask how they are doing. Sometimes they are struggling. Sometimes they are lonely. Sometimes they are dealing with health issues. Sometimes they are just happy to hear from someone who cares.

And sometimes, they simply feel encouraged knowing they matter to someone. What I consistently discover is this:
The response is almost always "I'm so glad you called. It was good talking to you."

By focusing on someone else, my own suffering decreases. My perspective changes. Connection replaces isolation. Service brings relief.

And without even realizing it, I am practicing several principles at once:

- Service (Step 12)
- Brotherly Love (Step 8)
- Spiritual Awareness (Step 11)
- Perseverance (Step 10)
- Humility (Step 7)

Isn't that amazing? One minute we are heading to the "pity pot", and the next we are transformed.

The Paradox of Service

One of the great paradoxes of spiritual life is this: When we help others, we help ourselves. Not because we are seeking personal benefit. But because service moves us out of self-centered thinking and into connection. And connection heals. Service does not have to be dramatic. It simply requires showing up.

Small acts matter:

A phone call.

A kind word.

Listening.

Encouragement.

Helping someone practically.

Being present.

These moments create meaning. And meaning creates joy.

A Life of Purpose

Over time, practicing these principles becomes natural. We begin living with intention. We look for opportunities to help. We respond with compassion more often. Purpose emerges not from grand achievements, but from daily choices. We become people who contribute.

And that changes everything.

Continued Growth

Step Twelve is not the end. Growth continues. We still practice awareness. We still seek connection. We still correct mistakes. Life remains dynamic.

But now we have tools.

Gratitude and Meaning

Many people discover deep gratitude along this journey. Gratitude for change. Gratitude for support. Gratitude for life itself. Purpose and gratitude reinforce each other.

The Ripple Effect

Positive change spreads. When we act with kindness, others respond. When we show patience, conflict decreases. When we share hope, hope grows.

Our transformation affects more than just us.

Putting Step Twelve into Practice

Step Twelve begins with simple willingness to contribute.

Ask yourself:

Who might benefit from my experience?

How can I support someone today?

Where can I practice kindness or patience?

What opportunities for service exist around me?

Small actions matter.

Exercise: Purpose Reflection

1. What growth have I experienced?

2. How might my experiences help others?

3. What forms of service feel meaningful to me?

4. How can I practice these principles daily?

Write honestly.

A Simple Step Twelve Statement

I am willing to share what I have learned and live with purpose.

Optional Prayer

God, help me be useful to others.

Guide me to share hope and kindness.

Help me live these principles every day.

Amen.

The Journey Continues

The Twelve Steps are not a destination.

They are a path.

A way of living with awareness, connection, responsibility, and purpose.

Life will still include challenges.

But we now face them differently.

With honesty.

With humility.

With courage.

With faith.

And most importantly — We do not walk alone.

The chains that once held us no longer define us. We are free to live. Free to grow.

Free to help others find the same freedom.

Epilogue
A New Way to Live

If someone had told me years ago that my life would one day become peaceful, meaningful, and full of purpose, I would have quietly dismissed them.

There was a time when I felt trapped.
Trapped by addiction. Trapped by fear.
Trapped by my own thinking.
I believed I had ruined too much. Lost too much.   Damaged too much.

But what I eventually discovered is something I hope every reader understands: Change is possible. Not instant change. Not perfect change.

But real change.

The kind that happens one decision at a time.

From Survival to Living

Before recovery, much of my life was about survival.

Avoid consequences.

Escape discomfort.

Control circumstances.

Numb emotions.

After working through the steps, something shifted. I began living instead of surviving. I developed awareness.
I learned responsibility. I discovered humility. I experienced connection with God.

I found purpose in helping others. Life did not become perfect. But it became meaningful. And meaning is far more powerful than comfort alone.

The Principles That Guide Me

The principles associated with the steps are not ideas I used once and moved beyond.

They are tools I still rely on every day.

Honesty when I want to hide.

Hope when I feel discouraged.

Faith when I feel uncertain.

Courage when I feel afraid.

Integrity when choices are difficult.

Willingness when resistance appears.

Humility when pride surfaces.

Brotherly love when relationships are strained.

Justice when I need accountability.

Perseverance when growth feels slow.

Spiritual awareness when life feels noisy.

Service when self-focus begins to creep in.

These principles continue to shape my life.

They can shape yours too.

Working the First Three Steps Every Day

One of the most important things I have learned is that I still have to work the first three steps every day.

There is a saying in recovery circles: The only step we have to do perfectly is the First Step.

We admitted we were powerless…

For me, that means more than admitting I am powerless over

alcohol — although that remains critically important. If I take a

drink, the drink will take me. I will lose control. And I may not

make it back. Many of us don't.

But Step One also means admitting I am powerless over many

other things in life.

People.

Places.

Things.

Situations.

Circumstances.

Life happens. People make choices. Unexpected events occur.

I am not in control of most of it.

And unless I want to drive myself crazy trying to control the

uncontrollable, I have to continue working Steps Two and

Three.

The Serenity Prayer

One tool that helps me tremendously is the Serenity Prayer:

God, grant me the serenity to accept the things I cannot change,

the courage to change the things I can,

and the wisdom to know the difference.

What can't I change?

Other people.

Past events.

Many circumstances.

Unexpected problems.

What can I change?

Me.

My attitude.

My actions.

My response.

Step Two reminds me that I have a Higher Power who can restore me to sanity. I don't have to spiral emotionally every time something goes wrong.

Step Three reminds me to turn my entire life — and my entire will — over to the care of God. When I do that, something remarkable happens. Wisdom begins to emerge naturally. Not perfectly. But consistently.

The more I practice acceptance and surrender, the more peaceful I become.

It is work.
But it is good work.

Accepting Life on Life's Terms

There is a joke that highlights the difference in perspective recovery can bring.
They say that if a non-alcoholic gets a flat tire, they simply call roadside assistance and have someone come fix it.
When an alcoholic gets a flat tire, they have to call the suicide prevention hotline.

It's funny — but it also contains truth. All of us, at times, struggle with accepting life on life's terms. We get frustrated. Angry. Overwhelmed.

Today, because of the Twelve Steps, I have a much better chance of responding differently. If I get a flat tire, I can pause and recognize something important: Things are exactly the way they are… in that moment.

God's will — not mine.

I accept what I cannot change. And then I change what I can. Ironically, in this example, I can change myself and my attitude…

And I can also change the tire.

That is the wisdom the prayer talks about.

And that wisdom grows the more we practice these steps every day.

Imperfection Is Part of the Journey

I still make mistakes. I still experience fear. Frustration. Self-doubt. But I recover more quickly now. I have tools. I have perspective. I have faith that growth continues.

And that makes all the difference.

Freedom Is Real

One of the greatest gifts of this process is freedom.

Freedom from constant self-judgment.

Freedom from resentment dominating my thoughts.

Freedom from living only for myself.

Freedom from feeling alone.

Freedom does not mean life has no problems.

It means our problems no longer define us..

You Do Not Have to Do This Alone

Whatever brought you to this book — struggle, curiosity, pain, growth, faith, or simply interest — I want you to know something important.

You are not alone.

Every human being wrestles with fear, doubt, mistakes, and uncertainty. The Twelve Steps offer a path that has helped millions — and they have helped me. They are not only for addiction.

They are for life.

An Invitation

If there is one message I hope you take with you, it is this:
You can begin where you are. You do not need to be perfect.
You do not need to have everything figured out. Small steps
matter. Honesty matters. Willingness matters. Connection
matters.

And over time, those small steps create profound change.

A Life Beyond Expectations

My life today is not what I planned. It is better. Not because
circumstances are always easy. But because I live differently.

With gratitude.

With purpose.

With connection.

With hope.

And that is available to anyone willing to walk this path.

The Journey Continues

The steps are not an ending. They are a beginning. A way of
living. A path of growth that continues for a lifetime. Every day
I am given another opportunity to practice these principles —
to accept, to grow, to serve, and to trust.

And wherever you are on that path, I am grateful you are here. The chains that once held us do not have to define us.

Freedom is possible. And you are worth the journey.

The journey of freedom is not completed in a single day. It unfolds one step at a time. Wherever you are today, remember that change is possible, hope is real, and a new way of living is always within reach.

A Personal Note About Recovery Programs

Before concluding this book, I want to make something clear.

I do not represent or speak on behalf of Alcoholics Anonymous or any other recovery program. I am simply sharing my own experience.

Alcoholics Anonymous has played a profound role in my life. Through the Twelve Steps and the fellowship of others in recovery, I found sobriety and a new way of living.

At the same time, my sobriety is ultimately my responsibility.

As the Big Book of Alcoholics Anonymous reminds us:
"We are not cured of alcoholism. What we really have is a daily reprieve contingent on the maintenance of our spiritual condition."

That statement has always been very real to me.
If someone were to hear that I had returned to drinking, it would not mean that Alcoholics Anonymous had failed. It

would mean that I had failed to maintain my spiritual condition. It would mean that I had stopped admitting my powerlessness over alcohol and stopped turning my life and my will over to God.

In other words, it would mean that I had once again decided that I was in control.

Experience has shown many of us where that path leads — back into the rooms of recovery, into institutions, into prison, or even into the cemetery.

But if I continue to practice these principles and live the Twelve Steps one day at a time, I have nothing to fear.

Because the promise of this way of life is real.

It is possible to live **happy, joyous, and free.**

Appendix A

The Twelve Steps

The following are the Twelve Steps as originally written in the program of Alcoholics Anonymous. Over time, many people have discovered that these principles apply not only to recovery from addiction, but to many areas of life where change and growth are needed.

1. We admitted we were powerless over alcohol—that our lives had become unmanageable.

2. Came to believe that a Power greater than ourselves could restore us to sanity.

3. Made a decision to turn our will and our lives over to the care of God as we understood Him.

4. Made a searching and fearless moral inventory of ourselves.

5. Admitted to God, to ourselves, and to another human being the exact nature of our wrongs.

6. Were entirely ready to have God remove all these defects of character.

7. Humbly asked Him to remove our shortcomings.

8. Made a list of all persons we had harmed, and became willing to make amends to them all.

9. Made direct amends to such people wherever possible, except when to do so would injure them or others.

10. Continued to take personal inventory and when we were wrong promptly admitted it.

11. Sought through prayer and meditation to improve our conscious contact with God as we understood Him, praying only for knowledge of His will for us and the power to carry that out.

12. Having had a spiritual awakening as the result of these steps, we tried to carry this message to others and to practice these principles in all our affairs.

The word "alcohol" appears only once in the Twelve Steps. Many people have found that the principles behind the Steps apply to many other struggles in life as well — fear, resentment, unhealthy habits, relationships, control, or patterns of thinking that keep us stuck.

As you reflect on these steps, you may find it helpful to consider the particular areas of life where you are seeking change, healing, or growth.

Appendix B

The Serenity Prayer

Reinhold Niebuhr

Short Version

God grant me the serenity
to accept the things I cannot change;
courage to change the things I can;
and wisdom to know the difference.
Full Version

God grant me the serenity
to accept the things I cannot change;
courage to change the things I can;
and wisdom to know the difference.

Living one day at a time;
enjoying one moment at a time;
accepting hardships as the pathway to peace;
taking, as He did, this sinful world
as it is, not as I would have it;
trusting that He will make all things right
if I surrender to His Will;
that I may be reasonably happy in this life
and supremely happy with Him
forever in the next. Amen.

Appendix C

Fourth Step Inventory

Resentments, Fears, and Harm Done to Others

The following guidance is based on the instructions found in the Alcoholics Anonymous Big Book. Readers are encouraged to review the relevant pages before beginning their inventory.

AA Big Book Online:
https://www.aa.org/the-big-book

———

Resentments

Before beginning, read from the bottom of **page 63 through page 65** in the Big Book.

Create a four-column inventory.

Column 1 — Resentments
List all people, places, things, institutions, ideas, or principles with whom you are angry, resentful, hurt, or feel threatened by.

Column 2 — The Cause

What happened? Be specific about why you were angry or resentful.

Column 3 — Affects My…
How did it make you feel? Specifically consider how the situation affected the Seven Parts of Self (listed below).

Column 4 — Where Was I to Blame?
Before answering, read the second paragraph on page 67.

Ask yourself honestly:

Where was my responsibility in this situation?
What part did I play?
What might I have done differently?

———

Fears

Read the Big Book, **page 67 (last paragraph) through the first paragraph on page 68**.

List your fears.

Then reflect on the following:

• Why do I have this fear?

• How has this fear affected my behavior?

• Has self-reliance failed me in this area?

———

Sexual Conduct / Harm Done to Others

Read carefully **pages 68–70** in the Big Book.

Make a list of situations involving sexual conduct or harm done to others.

Reflect on:

• What happened?
• What part did I play?
• How did my actions affect others?
• What could I have done differently?

The goal is honesty and awareness, not self-condemnation.

———

The Seven Parts of Self

These areas are often affected by resentments and fears.

Self-Esteem — How I think of myself

Pride — How I believe others see me

Pocketbook — Desire for money, possessions, or financial security

Personal Relations — My relationships with others

Ambition — My goals, plans, and future designs

Emotional Security — My sense of well-being and stability

Sex Relations — My desire for intimacy and connection

———

Additional Worksheets

Free Step Four worksheets are available online:

https://reidmyers.com/free-resources

Appendix D

The Daily Examen

Saint Ignatius of Loyola

The Daily Examen is a short reflective prayer developed by Saint Ignatius of Loyola. It is often practiced in the evening and typically takes only three to five minutes. The purpose of the Examen is to recognize God's presence throughout the day and to become more aware of how we are responding to that presence.

The Examen is traditionally practiced in five simple movements:

1. Become Aware of God's Presence
Quiet yourself and acknowledge that God is with you and has been present throughout your entire day.

2. Review the Day with Gratitude

Recall specific moments, gifts, and interactions from your day that brought joy or, in retrospect, revealed God's presence.

3. Pay Attention to Your Emotions

Reflect on the feelings you experienced during the day—peace, frustration, joy, anxiety, or gratitude. Notice which moments drew you closer to God and which pulled you away.

4. Choose One Moment and Pray

Focus on a specific moment from the day—either a high point or a struggle—and speak to God about it. Ask for forgiveness where needed or offer thanks for grace received.

5. Look Toward Tomorrow with Hope

Ask for God's guidance and grace for the day ahead. Consider how you hope to live tomorrow with greater awareness, patience, and trust.

Practiced regularly, the Examen helps cultivate spiritual awareness and gratitude in everyday life.

———

The Suscipe Prayer

Saint Ignatius of Loyola

Take, Lord, and receive all my liberty,

my memory, my understanding,

and my entire will.

All I have and call my own

you have given to me.

To you, Lord, I return it.

Everything is yours;

do with it what you will.

Give me only your love and your grace.

That is enough for me.

Suscipe is a Latin word meaning **"receive"** or **"take."**

Resources for Support and Growth

The journey toward healing, recovery, and personal growth does not have to be taken alone.
Support, guidance, and community are available.

If you are struggling or seeking support, the following organizations and resources may be helpful. Many offer confidential assistance, meetings, and information for individuals and families.

If you are in immediate danger or experiencing thoughts of self-harm, please seek help immediately. - CALL 988

———

Crisis Support

Suicide & Crisis Lifeline (U.S.)
Call or text 988

Available 24 hours a day, 7 days a week for anyone experiencing emotional distress or thoughts of suicide.

Website: https://988lifeline.org

———

Crisis Text Line

Text HOME to 741741

Free, confidential support via text message with trained crisis counselors.

Website: https://www.crisistextline.org

———

Recovery & Support Programs

Alcoholics Anonymous (AA)

AA is a worldwide fellowship of individuals who share their experience, strength, and hope with each other in order to solve their common problem and help others recover from alcoholism.

Website: https://www.aa.org

Find meetings: https://www.aa.org/find-aa

———

Narcotics Anonymous (NA)

NA is a community-based recovery organization for people struggling with drug addiction.

Website: https://www.na.org

Find meetings: https://www.na.org/meetingsearch

———

Overeaters Anonymous (OA)

OA offers a program of recovery for people struggling with compulsive eating behaviors.

Website: https://oa.org

Find meetings: https://oa.org/find-a-meeting

———

Sex Addicts Anonymous (SAA)

A fellowship of individuals who share their experience, strength, and hope to recover from addictive sexual behavior.

Website: https://saa-recovery.org

———

Al-Anon Family Groups

Support for families and friends affected by someone else's drinking.

Website: https://al-anon.org

———

Adult Children of Alcoholics (ACA)

Support for adults who grew up in alcoholic or dysfunctional family systems.

Website: https://adultchildren.org

———

Gamblers Anonymous

Support for individuals struggling with gambling addiction.

Website: https://www.gamblersanonymous.org

———

Alternative Recovery Programs

SMART Recovery

SMART Recovery offers a science-based approach to addiction recovery using tools from cognitive behavioral therapy and motivational methods.

Website: https://www.smartrecovery.org

Find meetings: https://meetings.smartrecovery.org

Abuse & Trauma Support

National Sexual Assault Hotline

Call 800-656-HOPE (4673)

Confidential support for survivors of sexual assault.

Website: https://www.rainn.org

———

National Domestic Violence Hotline

Call 800-799-SAFE (7233)
Text START to 88788

Website: https://www.thehotline.org

———

Mental Health Support

SAMHSA National Helpline

The Substance Abuse and Mental Health Services Administration (SAMHSA) offers confidential treatment referrals and information.

Call 1-800-662-HELP (4357)

Available 24 hours a day, 365 days a year.

Website: https://www.samhsa.gov/find-help/national-helpline

———

National Alliance on Mental Illness (NAMI)

NAMI provides education, advocacy, and support for individuals and families affected by mental illness.

Website: https://www.nami.org

———

Faith and Recovery

Catholic in Recovery

Catholic in Recovery integrates the Twelve Steps with Catholic spirituality and sacramental life.

Website: https://www.catholicinrecovery.com

———

Celebrate Recovery

Celebrate Recovery is a Christian-centered recovery program used in churches around the world to address addiction and other life struggles.

Website: https://www.celebraterecovery.com

———

Finding Local Support

Many communities offer local meetings, counseling services, recovery ministries, and support groups. If you are seeking help, consider reaching out to:

- **Local recovery meetings in your area**
- **Churches or faith communities that host recovery groups**
- **Licensed counselors or therapists**
- **Community health centers**
- **Hospital behavioral health programs**

If you are unsure where to begin, the websites listed above can help you locate meetings and support groups in your area.

———

Worksheets and Additional Materials

Worksheets and reflection tools referenced in this book are available for free download at:

www.reidmyers.com/resources

These materials include:

• Step Four inventory worksheets
• Personal reflection exercises
• Prayer and meditation guides
• Additional tools for working the Twelve Steps

These resources are provided to help readers continue exploring the principles discussed in this book.

———

Continuing the Journey

Personal growth and recovery are ongoing journeys. Many people find encouragement through community, shared stories, and continued learning.

Additional resources, music, and inspirational materials from the author can be found at:

www.reidmyers.com

Information about Keynote Concerts, presentations, and speaking events is also available there for churches, recovery groups, and community organizations.

A Final Word

Seeking help is a sign of courage, not weakness. Many people have walked this path before you, and many are ready to walk beside you now.

You do not have to do this alone.
Support, hope, and community are available.

About the Author

Reid Myers is a speaker, musician, minister, and recovery advocate who shares a message of hope, personal growth, and spiritual renewal through music, storytelling, and practical wisdom.

After overcoming his own battle with alcoholism and experiencing the life-changing impact of the Twelve Steps, Reid is dedicated to helping others find freedom, purpose, and peace. Drawing from his personal journey, years of recovery, and experience in ministry, he speaks and performs for churches, recovery communities, conferences, and special events.

Through his Keynote Concerts, Reid combines music, personal stories, humor, and insight to inspire audiences and encourage meaningful change. His presentations focus on recovery, faith, resilience, and the universal principles found within the Twelve Steps.

In addition to keynote presentations, Reid offers workshops, webinars, and personal life coaching designed to help individuals apply these principles in everyday life. His programs focus on personal growth, overcoming adversity, emotional resilience, leadership, and living with greater purpose.

Reid also brings these same principles into corporate and business environments, where themes such as responsibility, integrity, humility, perseverance, and service can strengthen leadership, teamwork, and workplace culture. His presentations help organizations explore how timeless principles can support both personal well-being and professional effectiveness.

Reid lives in Kentucky with his wife, Catherine. They have been married for more than four decades and are blessed with two sons and several grandchildren.In addition to writing and speaking, Reid continues to share his message through music, teaching, and outreach.

For information about Keynote Concerts and additional resources, visit: www.reidmyers.com

If you are ready for real change...
this is your next step.

Breaking the Patterns: Coaching

This is where we go beyond awareness—and begin real transformation.

- A personalized plan tailored to your specific challenges
- Weekly accountability and follow-up
- Clear steps that break big goals into achievable progress
- Support, guidance, and encouragement rooted in experience and hope

This is a safe, judgment-free space where you can explore your challenges, gain clarity, and take practical steps toward lasting change—at your own pace.

It starts with a Free Discovery Session.

We'll talk about where you are, where you want to go, and whether this is the right fit for you. From there, you can choose the level of support that fits your needs and your goals.

To Book Your Free Discovery Session Go To:

www.reidmyers.com/life-coaching

Bring Reid Myers to Your Event

The message in Breaking the Chains That Bind Us began long before this book was written.

For many years, Reid Myers has shared this message through music, storytelling, and keynote presentations that explore the life-changing principles of the Twelve Steps and the power of spiritual growth.

Through a unique combination of inspiring music, personal experience, humor, and practical wisdom, Reid helps audiences discover how the principles of recovery can be applied to everyday life — offering hope, clarity, and tools for lasting change.

Reid's keynote concerts and workshops are designed to encourage reflection, personal growth, and renewed purpose. Audiences often describe these events as both deeply meaningful and highly engaging.

Events can be tailored for a wide variety of audiences, including:

• Churches and faith communities

• Recovery groups and conferences

• Retreats and spiritual gatherings

• Corporate and workplace events

• Community organizations

• Schools and universities

Programs may include:

Keynote Concert Presentations
Music, storytelling, and inspiration that bring the principles of recovery and personal transformation to life.

Breaking the Chains Workshops
Interactive sessions that help participants identify the "chains" that hold them back and learn practical tools for growth, freedom, and emotional resilience.

Retreats and Special Events
Extended sessions designed for deeper reflection, discussion, and spiritual renewal.
If you would like to bring this message to your community, organization, or event, you can learn more or make an inquiry contact: reid@musicbyreid.com

www.reidmyers.com